Three of China's Mighty Men

by

LESLIE LYALL

D1580626

OMF BOOKS ◇ LONDON

First published October 1973

The simplified, romanized Chinese script, now widely in use, has been adopted in this book, except in the case of some names which would thereby be made unfamiliar.

ISBN 85363 090 9

Made in Great Britain

Published by Overseas Missionary Fellowship
Newington Green, London, N16 9QD
and printed by the Camelot Press Ltd., London and Southampton

Contents

Part 3 WANG MING-DAO: Man of Iron

Three of
CHINA'S MIGHTY MEN

". . . the mighty men whom David had"
2 Samuel 23.8

David's Mighty Men

King David drew to himself, both in his wilderness days when life was dangerous and in his years on the throne of Israel, many loyal followers—his mighty men. Three were outstanding for their magnificent courage, their single-handed victories, their reckless defiance of the national enemies and their sacrificial willingness to risk life itself to bring satisfaction to their royal master.

Like David's guerilla force in his years of exile, the Church of Jesus Christ in China has always been a small minority, struggling for its survival against enormous odds. Yet in her comparatively short history, she has produced her mighty men who have been drawn to Christ from Confucianism and Buddhism, from atheism and materialism. They have loyally and courageously served Him with a sacrificial spirit unexcelled in any period of the Church's history. These men and women were found in every branch of the Christian Church from the earliest days to the present.

Of the less than one million Christians in all the Protestant churches in 1949 those which were the fruit of the work of the China Inland Mission (89,665) numbered second only to those associated with the Church of Christ in China (166,660), a union of fourteen churches including Presbyterian, Methodist, Congregationalist and Baptist. The True Jesus Church came third with 80,000 and the Little

Flock (Assembly Hall) fifth with 70,000.[1] It is not
generally recognized that Christians belonging to
the three independent movements—True Jesus
Church, Little Flock and Jesus Family—together
with the China Inland Mission Christians totalled
one-quarter of the entire Protestant church membership in China.

It would be invidious to single out three men
among all the churches as chief among Christ's
mighty men in China. The author is not qualified to
write about the many outstanding leaders in the
Church of Christ, the Episcopal churches in China
and the many other smaller churches. But in the
China Inland Mission and independent churches
three names do stand out, not for their prominence
among China's Christian scholars nor their contribution in the wider affairs of society and the state, but
for their unique ability to expound the truths of
Holy Scripture, their profound influence on the
Chinese Church in an age of revolution and their
unflinching loyalty to "great David's greater Son".
The author counts it a privilege to have known each
of the three as friends and two of them as co-workers
in the work of evangelism and church planting. But
in reporting as faithfully as possible the views they
held and the attitudes they adopted towards other
churches in China he does not necessarily endorse
or commend them.

The following pages tell in brief the stories of
Yang Shao-t'ang of Shansi, Nee Duo-sheng of
Shanghai, and Wang Ming-dao of Peking—three
contemporaries who made their mark in different
ways on the Church in China.

[1] *World Christian Handbook, 1949.* Ed. Sir Kenneth G. Grubb.

PART 1

YANG SHAO-T'ANG

Man of Humility

1 *Tragedy in the North*

"They've killed them all!"

"Who?"

"The Boxers have killed Pastor and Mrs. Kay and the little girl!"

For eleven years the Kays had lovingly and faithfully proclaimed the Good News about Jesus Christ throughout the district of Quwo. Mr. and Mrs. Kay of the China Inland Mission spoke Chinese fluently and Mr. Kay filled his preaching with copious illustrations taken from local life. As the church he planted grew, he started a school for Christian children which soon achieved a high reputation for its tone, excellent discipline and good scholarship. The Kays were greatly beloved by all.

But the last years of the nineteenth century had been marred by a growing hostility towards all foreigners on account of the way in which the Western powers were exploiting a defenceless China. Humiliation followed humiliation until, in 1900, national feelings reached boiling point. Shansi Province was more seriously affected than others and forty-two missionaries and their children were to lose their lives there, as well as many faithful Chinese Christians. In June anti-foreign riots broke out in Taiyuan, the capital, where mission buildings were burned to the ground, and at Pingyao and Jiehxiu. When escape from the province for the Kays seemed impossible, the local Christians, who would have done anything to secure their safety, advised the Kay family to hide in the country. So they took refuge in the Taho mountains forty miles south-east of the city. As soon as they had left the city the magistrate sealed their home, but his underlings pilfered their possessions. Eventually Mr. and Mrs. Kay and their daughter were captured by the Boxers and brought back to Quwo. There, one hot summer day in August, they died, presumably decapitated with Boxer swords as others were.

The Christians were stunned. But almost immediately they found themselves in danger as the Boxers looted and set fire to Christian homes in the city and villages. Among the families threatened was the Yang family in the village of that name. Farmer Yang had been one of the first Christian converts in the district. Amid the terror and sorrow of that fateful "Year of the Rat", a son was born to the Yang family to bring them comfort and joy.

The province of Shansi ("West of the Mountains") lies four hundred miles inland from the China Sea, enfolded by the muddy waters of the Yellow River. It is commonly known as the "cradle of Chinese civilization". There the first of the Han race from somewhere far to the west had settled. There lived the mythical emperors of China's "Golden Age", Yao and Shun, and ancient temples bear their names and perpetuate their memory. It was there that Fu-hsi, the discoverer (and god) of Chinese herbal medicines, made his first experiments. There too Yu was deputed by Yao to release the flood waters of the Yellow River and never once went home to his newly-wed bride until the task was completed—the classical model of devotion to duty.

In the north of the province are the scenically

magnificent Wu-tai Shan ("Mountains of the Five Peaks"), a famed Buddhist centre where 10,000 monks used to serve a thousand well-kept and spectacular temples; these were the object of an annual religious fair visited by thousands of devout Buddhist pilgrims from Tibet and Mongolia. Throughout the centre of the province flows the Fen River along whose fertile banks lie most of the main cities. The rich loess soil covers the underlying rocks to a great depth, but artesian wells everywhere provide water for irrigation—a good thing, for rain only falls during a month or two in high summer, transfiguring a dry, golden landscape into tropical luxuriance and the ancient deeply sunken cart-roads into quagmires. The mountains east and west of the Fen River are comparatively barren but even there the industrious inhabitants living in their cave homes, hewn out of the loess cliffs, eke out an existence. Beneath the surface of Shansi lies one of the richest coal fields in China, scarcely worked at all until the Communists gained power.

The people of Shansi are hardy and hard working. In the long winter their gowns and trousers are padded with cotton or camel's hair or lined with sheep-skin, while fur hats and ear-muffs protect them from the bitter winds blowing from the frozen Gobi Desert to the north.

The first notable convert to Christianity in this province was a Confucian scholar by the name of Hsi who took the "Christian" name of Sheng-mo, or "Conqueror of Demons". He is generally known as Pastor Hsi. He had been an opium addict when he entered a literary competition for the best essay in classical style on the subject of Jesus as portrayed in Mark's Gospel. The study of the Gospel led to Hsi's

conversion and effected a radical transformation in
his life, including the breaking of his opium addiction.
The erstwhile Confucian scholar now became an
evangelist and a church-planter. In city after city
along the banks of the Fen River, in the mountains
to the east and west he won converts, helped the
opium addicts to break their addiction and founded
churches. It was to these churches that several members of the Cambridge Seven, who had come to
China under the China Inland Mission, ministered
for many years, notably D. E. Hoste, the ex-Royal
Artillery officer, C. T. Studd, the England cricketer,
and Stanley Smith, member of the Cambridge boat.

The 1900 crisis over, and thanks to the generous
attitude of the China Inland Mission in not accepting
any indemnity for the loss of life and property, the
attitude of the Chinese to missionaries changed and
churches multiplied. Subsequently hospitals were
opened in Taiyuan-fu by Lord Rochdale and by the
China Inland Mission in Linfen within whose ancient
walls was a great temple named after the Emperor
Yao, and at Changzhi over the mountains to the
east. A Bible School was started in Linfen but later
moved twenty miles north to the prosperous little
town of Hongdong, irrigated by a perennial supply
of water from a river bursting out of the nearby
mountain. And in the 1920s on a hill outside the
Hongdong city walls, a splendid High School was
built in memory of D. E. Hoste, Pastor Hsi's close
friend and co-worker. Pastor Hsi and his devoted
wife continued to live in a village of Linfen County.
Thirty years after the Boxer tragedy the Christian
Church was a flourishing and witnessing reality.

2 *A Farmer's Son*

The little Yang baby of Yang-jia-juang (the Yang
family village) in Quwo grew up in the atmosphere
of a Christian home. All around were the village
temples and shrines which did not lack for devotees.
The seasons passed and the Chinese calendar was
an accurate guide to the activities of the farm, for
this ancient calendar had been compiled in this very
province from long and careful observation of the
climate. February saw the "Beginning of Spring"
and "Rain-water", followed by "Excited Insects" in
March. The "Clear and Bright" Festival was in
April when the apricot blossoms splashed the bare
hillsides with colour, and when everyone except the
Christians used to visit the ancestral graves to make
their offerings there. As the sun became warmer
"Grain Rains", "Grain Fills" and "Grain in Ear"
followed. In June, the busiest time of the year
for him and all in his village, Farmer Yang
harvested his winter wheat and sowed his autumn
cereals—millet, sorgum millet and maize. "Summer
Solstice" was followed by "Slight Heat", then "Great
Heat" accompanied by thunderstorms and heavy
rain. "Start of Autumn" began on August 7th;
"White Dew" followed on September 8th with "Cold
Dew" a month later. Soon it was "Hoar Frost
Descends", and old Mrs. Yang would take the
precaution of moving her pot plants indoors before
October 23rd. Finally, in succession came "Winter

B

Begins", "Little Snow", "Heavy Snow", "Little
Cold", "Severe Cold". The land was once more in
the grip of hard winter and the Yang family and
everyone else in Yang-jia-juang hugged the warmth
of the "k'ang"—the flue-heated brick platform
which is both a family bed and a family sitting-room.

As the little Yang family heir reached school age
he exchanged his baby name for Shao-t'ang, the
name by which he would be known for the rest of his
life, though later he adopted the Christian name of
David. His was a happy childhood and at the local
Christian primary school David learned to love the
Bible. At twelve years of age he moved on to the
provincial Christian Middle School at Hongdong.
The impressive buildings in Chinese architectural
style but with modern design and even central
heating made a country boy feel a little strange at
first, but he was one of many leading church workers
who received their education and Christian character
training at the Hoste School. During David's time
there the headmaster was Rowland Hogben, a stern
but deeply respected teacher from England.

Life at the school was varied. Educationally, the
standards were high and the discipline strict but
basket-ball, football and athletics played a large part
in the school programme. Once a year there was a
school outing to the famous Kwang Sheng Si Springs,
whence Hongdong and its neighbour city, Wanan
(Chaocheng), derived their fertility. The annual fair
to honour the god of the springs was also a good
opportunity for evangelism, in which staff and boys
took part. David was given a solid grounding in the
Christian life at Hongdong and showed unusual
promise.

The local Bible School catered largely for the less

well educated, and only trained evangelists. David's aim was the Christian ministry, and the best evangelical theological college in North China was the Presbyterian Seminary at Tengxian in the neighbouring province of Shantung. So with the help of his parents and the churches of Shansi David began his study at Tengxian in 1923.

3 *A Spiritual Turning Point*

China was still reeling from the effects of the Versailles Peace Treaty which had given her old enemy Japan special privileges on China's soil and the territory which had previously been a German possession. Earlier, Japan had made her humiliating twenty-one demands on China, so China, especially the student world, was seething with anti-Japanese agitation and conducting a boycott of all Japanese imports. The Chinese Communist Party had been formed in 1921 and was becoming very active; its propaganda was specious and effective. But simultaneously God was demonstrating His power. The churches in Shantung were experiencing revival and indeed all over China the message of revival was being proclaimed by the Bethel Bands, who had their headquarters in Shanghai, and by missionaries like Miss Marie Monsen of Norway. Almost inevitably this movement of revival took some wrong turnings; the false and the spurious were there to deceive the untaught and the unwary and there were Satanic counterfeits of the Holy Spirit's working. It was both a time of spiritual renewal and a time of considerable confusion.

At Tengxian David Yang was also confused. When people asked his opinion about the "Spiritual Grace Society" (which placed an exaggerated emphasis on "spiritual" gifts), the "Holy Spirit Society" or the "True Jesus Church", all of which with their new emphasis on the work of the Holy Spirit were causing controversy, David had no authoritative answer, because he had no deep personal experience of his own. But realizing his future responsibilities as a pastor and leader he was determined to seek out the truth for himself.

In the summer vacation of 1924 the seminary sent him to the beautiful mountain resort of Kuling, south of the Yangtze in the province of Kiangsi, to attend a convention for the deepening of spiritual life. There he listened to many celebrated preachers including a missionary who spoke about the problems of spiritual experience.

"I did not pay much attention because I was confident that I was a saved man. From a child I had received an excellent religious education and I sincerely believed. Moreover I was training at a theological college in preparation for serving the Lord in the future. How could it be that I was not saved? Nevertheless I asked the Lord not to let me return to college empty-handed. So, besides listening to the addresses I was busy writing up my notes. But, praise the Lord, when I did not even know what grace was, in my weakness and ignorance the Lord saved me. There came to me a burden of sin which so weighed upon me and bound me that I said to myself, 'If the Lord's power to save is so limited and so insufficient to give me peace and deliverance then

I really doubt if Jesus is alive at all.' But thanks to my gracious Lord Jesus, early on the morning of the 7th of July He found this lost sheep. The blood of the Cross flowed into my heart and the burden of sin fell away. For the very first time I enjoyed a true relationship with Jesus Christ and from that day until now the Lord has continued to do His marvellous work in my life."

4 *Times of Testing*

After graduation in 1925 David Yang refused offers of well-paid Presbyterian pastorates and decided to return to his home province of Shansi to serve the Lord there. Trials of many kinds awaited him, not least the question of his livelihood. He was several times tempted to return to the Presbyterian area for financial security and was even persuaded once or twice that it might be God's will for him to leave Shansi. But God showed him clearly that his place of witness was to be Shansi and that only the place of God's appointment was the place where a servant can experience his Master's presence and blessing. He learned to fear getting out of God's will. "If the Lord is with me, though I pass through the valley of the shadow of death how blessed it will be."

David Yang's sphere of service was the thirteen churches in the thirteen counties of which Quwo, his native place, was to be his base. He was also pastor of the local church. Two lady missionaries of the China Inland Mission were in full sympathy and

fellowship with him in spiritual things. His extensive
"parish" frequently took him away from Quwo to
conduct local church conferences and district summer
conventions. The area was almost entirely rural,
though one larger city boasted a textile factory.
Travel was either by bus along the few dusty main
roads, on mule-back or by Peking cart to the more
remote places. It was not until 1934 that a railway
line was constructed between Taiyuan, the capital,
and Tong-guan on the Yellow River one hundred
miles to the south. The population and therefore the
Christians were largely simple farming folk or
merchants. The older generation had had little
education and the younger generation were seldom
educated beyond higher primary school.

In 1926 the evacuation of all missionaries to
the coast was made necessary by a nationwide,
Communist-inspired anti-foreign and anti-Christian
movement. The China Inland Mission, as soon as the
crisis was over in 1928, reading the signs of the times,
began to implement a policy of self-government,
self-support and self-propagation in place of missionary control for its churches all over China.
Hitherto missionaries had in many cases virtually
been the church pastors, while national evangelists,
Bible women and pastors (if there were any) and
school teachers had been subsidized by Mission
funds. For this reason the Communists called them
"running dogs of the imperialists". Now all was to be
different and the churches were expected to stand
on their own feet administratively and economically,
while the missionaries took a back seat. This policy
was not easily accepted by many simple Christians
who had been contented with the old paternalistic
situation. Most of them were poor; how could they

then be expected to assume financial responsibility for pastors, evangelists, teachers and Bible women? Lacking support, not a few Chinese evangelists decided to leave Shansi for church areas where such hard conditions were unknown and where foreign missions still paid handsome salaries to their workers. Such was the situation in which David Yang found himself—co-operating with the C.I.M. leadership in implementing these policies, while knowing full well he could be living comfortably elsewhere. In 1931 financial necessity and the need of the Hongdong High School took him there to be the Principal. He was already on the Board of Governors. In 1934 David Yang was actually invited to join the staff of the Tengxian Seminary, his Alma Mater, but he declined, for God was revealing to him His pattern of work for the future.

That same year Howard Knight was recalled from Kansu in the north-west to be the Vice-Principal at the Hoste School. In the north-west he had developed considerable cynicism about Chinese Christians who in those remote parts were mostly illiterate and had a comparatively low level of Christian experience. To an ardent young New Zealander they hardly seemed to be Christian in anything but name. Transferring to Shansi he did not expect to find the situation any different. But to his amazement and shame he found in David Yang a man of spiritual stature whose ministry was both deep and enriching. Here at last was a magnificent product of missionary work in China, a man at whose feet one could sit and learn of Christ. That young missionary, who was destined one day to become the Home Director of the China Inland Mission in Australia, was never quite the same again. For David Yang possessed a

radiant personality. His naturally plain face shone
with an inward joy. He was a simple but at the same
time skilful expositor of Scripture. The truths he
taught were deep but the language and the illustrations were such that the simplest Shansi Christians
could take them in. He loved to draw on home
relationships and farming life to give point to his
teaching. He knew the circumstances and the
spiritual problems of his people for he was one of
them and had the gift of making eternal truths living
and relevant to their Christian lives. No eloquent
evangelist like his friend Wang Ming-dao of Peking
(Beijing), he was yet a great teacher of the Scriptures.
And many a missionary today is grateful to God for
the ministry of David Yang.

In the early '30s echoes of revival in Shantung
were heard in Shansi. One of David Yang's Quwo
missionary co-workers, Miss Elizabeth Fischbacher,
went to Shantung to observe the revival for herself
and returned with a powerful and attractive new
message. In 1931 and 1932 Andrew Gih and Dr.
John Sung of the Bethel Worldwide Evangelistic
Band held successful campaigns in some of Shansi's
main cities. Chinese Christians and missionaries alike
experienced personal revival. It was not quite so hard
now for the Chinese churches to see the wisdom of
becoming utterly dependent on the Lord instead of
being half-dependent on a foreign missionary
organization. They even heartily desired to be truly
autonomous. Revival also added a spiritual impetus
to reaching out in evangelism. But a solution of the
manpower problem in the churches was not yet in
sight. Even the Hongdong Bible Institute students
could scarcely be expected to serve the churches of
their own province under existing conditions. Many

were asking whether there was not something far
from ideal about current church–mission relationships. Was there not some better way ahead for the
Shansi churches?

5 *A Growing Vision*

David Yang was carrying a very heavy burden
almost alone. He constantly wrestled with God in
prayer. Then, on one of his journeys, rain turned
the motor road into an impassable quagmire and
David had to spend several days in an inn waiting
for the weather to clear and the roads to dry. It was
in that crude hostelry that a clear vision of something
quite new came to him—that of a team of fellow
workers living a communal life of faith. Half of the
year they would devote to the study of the Bible and
the nature of the Christian ministry, and the other
half of the year they would go out in small teams to
minister to the churches and to evangelize, putting
into effect the truths learned while studying together.
Young missionaries would be welcome as members
of the team on a basis of complete equality with
their Chinese colleagues. The final pattern of things
became clear during a prolonged time of prayer and
it was for this reason that the answer to the Tengxian
Seminary invitation was "No". The "Ling Gong
Tuan" (Spiritual Action Team) was born. David's
main co-worker, a gifted Bible woman, also gave up
the thought of leaving Shansi in order to join Pastor
Yang in this new venture.

Meanwhile David Yang, faced with this new challenge, was deeply concerned about another important matter, namely "the fulness of the Holy Spirit". He was well aware that it would be "not by might, nor by power, but by my Spirit" that he could accomplish anything for God. This was not the first time that David had known this concern. He had thought and read about the subject a good deal. Once he wrote, "I sincerely and with faith received and the Lord did a gracious work in my heart. Afterwards, in all directions the Lord's power was truly present, but still I dared not confidently say that I had obtained His fulness. At times my heart was truly dissatisfied."

During the early summer of 1934, on land donated for the purpose, a cluster of simple buildings constructed of adobe went up, surrounding a central building to be used both for lectures and as a refectory. There were thirty-four rooms in all and everything was completed in just three months. In September twenty men and women who formed the Spiritual Action Team commenced their studies. Their prior aim, however, in preparation for Christian service was to seek "power from on high". "As for myself," wrote David Yang, the leader, "the more I sought, the farther away I seemed to be and into my mind there came a number of insoluble questions, some of them posed by Mr. Watchman Nee's book, *The Spiritual Man*." This book gave warnings about deceiving spirits and counterfeits, subjective or "soulish" experiences. But one thing emerged and that was that not to be filled with the Spirit was sin and disobedience to the command of God in Ephesians 5.18. So, putting aside all fears of Satanic deception and believing God would not allow him to be deceived, he earnestly sought God's fulness. Only when he himself had solved this problem once for all could he hope to help others to avoid the faults and discover the true experience.

It happened that a Spirit-filled pastor by the name of John Sun was conducting the Southern District Leaders' Retreat at Quwo that winter, and David Yang went to join them. A group of ten or so missionaries had already been meeting for prayer during the previous few days during which prejudice and jealousy had been burnt up, pride and self-assurance changed into child-likeness and all had been melted together by the fire of love. David Yang recognized this to be a true work of God and when the leaders' retreat began he took the lead. During the meetings one after another definitely experienced a filling of the Holy Spirit, some, but not all, speaking in tongues. On the third day, David decided to spend the whole day in prayer together with a few Chinese and missionary brothers and sisters, all of whom shared the same sense of need.

"Praise to our Father God, just after 4 p.m. the problem of my heart was absolutely and clearly solved. As we knelt praying God's Spirit showed me clearly for what I should seek . . . Previously I had received the fulness . . . but lacked the release of the Spirit. So I committed myself utterly to Him. Praise God, at once Malachi 4.2—'But unto you . . . shall the Sun of righteousness arise with healing in his wings'—illumined my heart and I rested completely in the rays of the Sun of Righteousness, allowing them to heal me. I was hardly conscious of being in the room, so conscious was I of being under the shadow of His wings. Suddenly the fetters of the flesh were loosed; my outlook was changed and

I knew a great power. It was no longer a question
of 'labour' and 'sacrifice' but everlasting rest (cf.
Isaiah 30.15) . . . These truths I had read about
before in books and mentally I had grasped them,
but it was not until now that I laid hold of them in
my own experience. Now at last I realized in my
heart a natural, living faith . . . Previously, though I
had been filled with much joy and praise I had been
unable to give expression to them. I could only
whisper 'praise the Lord'. Finally the Spirit of joy
flooded my breast and in a loud voice I shouted
'Hallelujah'. Power immediately filled my whole
body and up from my heart into my mouth I was
filled with praise. Joy, like the waves of the sea,
flowed forth and I laughed without restraint."

During that retreat the Lord did a deep work in
the hearts of many. It was no short-lived revival, for
living waters began to pour forth and those present
returned to their homes to witness in a new way to
their gracious Lord Jesus. A little while later Miss
Fischbacher held a Bible School in Quwo and another
leader was so greatly blessed that living waters began
to flow in his village and a number of heathen were
converted. The blessing spread to the Hongdong
Bible Institute where Miss Fischbacher also held
meetings. Many students and missionaries received
afresh or for the first time the Holy Spirit's fulness.
Speaking in tongues was not the common evidence
of the fulness, although in some cases this sign was
given. "Just now," says David Yang, "I can think of
a large number of brothers and sisters who three or
four months ago were weak and powerless yet today
have become strong leaders in the firing line, to
whom the Lord is entrusting the care of saved men
and women. . . . The living water still flows and I

believe that the Lord will give yet greater grace so that His Name might be glorified."

That prayer was answered and the Spiritual Action Team, which included several young missionaries, who were later to become leaders in the China Inland Mission, developed into a centre of rich spiritual life and activity. Faith had found a way. The problem of Spirit-filled workers for the revived churches promised to be solved. Missionaries rejoiced in the way God was taking things out of their hands. During that spring of 1935 the future on the spiritual scene looked very bright.

David Adeney, one of the young missionaries in the Spiritual Action Team, recalls those days:

"During my first years in Honan, China, when I was in my early twenties, David Yang used to visit Honan to speak at church conferences. I found him to be a truly humble man of God, able to expound the Scriptures with authority and spiritual power. I was so impressed that I felt I must spend a longer time with him. Hearing about the 'Ling Gong Tuan' in Shansi I asked permission to visit this Spiritual Action Team where both men and women joined together in study and evangelism, living as one family. Right at the centre of this fellowship was David Yang, the man who led us in the study of the Scriptures and in a deep fellowship with the Lord and with one another. He encouraged us to seek for a deeper understanding of the work of the Holy Spirit in our lives and of the gifts He has given to His Church. I can never forget a half-day spent in prayer when the truth of Ephesians 1.18–23 became clearer to me personally. David Yang himself was always trying to attain to a deeper fellowship with the Son of God. He had asked me to go and spend some time with him in prayer. I found him stretched out upon the mud floor of his simple room crying to God, confessing his own weakness and sinfulness and asking for cleansing and the filling of the Holy Spirit. He was already a man whose life was characterized by humility and Christlikeness and yet that day I saw him humbling himself before the Lord. It made an indelible impression upon me. I realized that however greatly a man might be used in the service of the Lord Jesus he is nevertheless constantly in need of repentance and of waiting upon God."

6 *War Clouds*

But clouds were darkening on the political horizon. The Communist armies had already completed their "Long March" from South to North China and in the spring of 1936 they crossed the Yellow River into Shansi and pillaged the countryside in search of silver and gold to refill their depleted coffers. They actually attacked several cities, like Hongdong which had twenty or more missionaries within its walls, but without much success. The Team premises at Houma were unmolested beyond having anti-Japanese slogans painted on their walls.

This new Communist advance sounded the alarm for the Japanese who were already in control of Manchuria and Peking. Events moved fast. The first shots of the Sino-Japanese War were fired outside Peking in July 1937 at the Marco Polo Bridge. It was not long before Shansi, for the second time in the half-century, was to experience a blood bath as the Japanese armies marched through pillaging, raping and torturing. Now the once peaceful Fen River valley and the enveloping mountains became the arena for warring armies—Japanese, Nationalist and Communist. In 1939 the Japanese burned the Spiritual Action Team premises to the ground, and forced the Team to disband. Its members scattered to their own homes and churches, some to lose their lives at Japanese hands. Others, however, subsequently became invaluable servants of God in different parts of China.

In view of the unceasing dangers, from guerilla activities in South Shansi against the Japanese, David Yang first took his family north to the comparative security of Taiyuan, the provincial capital. Then he moved to Tientsin (Tianjin) and finally to Peking for the duration of the Sino-Japanese war. There he conducted a modified version of the Spiritual Action Team—an informal Bible School. In Peking he was brought into closer fellowship with Mr. Wang Ming-dao, the well-known pastor of the Christian Tabernacle. Mr. Wang was a preacher in nation-wide demand as a conference speaker, the author of many popular books and the editor of a magazine which exercised a far-reaching influence on readers everywhere. David Yang was one of the few men whom Wang Ming-dao freely invited to occupy his pulpit. In Peking David Yang was also in close touch with Dr. John Sung[1] who was living and teaching in the Western Hills, though now a sick man after his years of exhausting travel and

[1] See *Flame for God: John Sung and Revival in the Far East* by Leslie Lyall.

evangelism. He died in 1944 and Mr. Wang Ming-dao conducted the funeral service.

Once the war with Japan was over, David Yang paid a return visit to his native province, war-torn and suffering, and now largely occupied by Communist forces. He presided at an enthusiastic provincial delegates' conference in Hongdong at which most of the thirty-eight counties of the former C.I.M. field were represented. The delegates gave David Yang a warm invitation to return permanently as the senior pastor or "bishop" for the whole area. But the recrudescence of civil war between the Nationalists and the Communists made it impossible to bring his wife and three children into such an uncertain and threatening situation.

In 1947 the leaders of the China Inland Mission in Shanghai invited David Yang to address a special gathering at their Sinza Road headquarters on the subject of Mission-Church relationships. The old paternalistic system had already been abandoned in 1928 but in enforcing a "self-supporting, self-governing, self-propagating" policy in the churches an unhappy dichotomy had sometimes developed. There were those who repeated, "The Mission is the Mission and the Church is the Church", as though the two things were poles apart. This was a case of over-reaction against an outmoded paternalism. During the war, under Bishop F. Houghton's leadership, a new policy had been formulated whereby the Mission's activities would be channelled through the local churches. This was a necessary correction of a policy which had swung too far away from missionary control over the churches. Now missionaries would only return if invited to do so and would function within the framework of the local church and under its leadership. David Yang warmly approved this new relationship. Unlike Watchman Nee, whose influence in the country was great and who never ceased to regard missionary societies and denominational churches as sectarian, David Yang was glad to work together with all who would serve on the Scriptural basis of the local church and who would follow the New Testament pattern of church life. David had been brought up in a "C.I.M." church and served in a "C.I.M." field and continued to feel a warm kinship with the C.I.M. and its ministry to the Chinese people.

7 *Growing Influence and Responsibility*

From Peking David Yang moved south at the invitation of the China Bible Seminary in Jiangwan, in the outer suburbs of Shanghai, to be a lecturer. When he also accepted a call to become pastor of the Huang Ni Gang church in Nanking (Nanjing) he moved his home there. This entailed constant travel backwards and forwards between Nanking and Shanghai.

David Yang was now in his prime and was able to draw from his long and varied experience in working out his convictions about local church life. This work in Nanking became very dear to his heart and the people grew very fond of their teacher and friend. But when in 1948 David was invited to become a full-time staff member of the China Bible Seminary he and his family moved house once again to

C

Shanghai. The Seminary was possibly the best of all the independent Bible Schools in China. Its standard was high and its graduates had earned a reputation throughout China for their spiritual qualities. Many had reached out as missionaries to remote areas of their own land and were performing stalwart service for God everywhere—in the south-west and in the north-west, even in Turkestan.

At Jiangwan David Yang's rich exposition of the Scriptures and godly wisdom contributed greatly to making the China Bible Seminary a place of even more vital spiritual training for the many young men and women who came under his influence.

During the winter and summer vacations he was usually away attending student conferences in Nanking, Peking and elsewhere. God was at work in a new way among university students everywhere. From every university centre news was accumulating of conversions and of revival. Hundreds were turning to Christ and were seeking the deeper things of Christian experience. Men like Pastor David Yang and Mr. Wang Ming-dao were able to an unusual extent to meet that need. In 1948 the second All-China Conference of Evangelical Students met in Nanking. It was an unforgettable occasion. The participants came from all parts of China, by sea, by air or by rail. David Yang was the chief speaker. It proved to be the last such conference, but during those memorable days three hundred young men and women were fired with the desire to dedicate their whole lives to Christ as living witnesses, whatever the future might hold and however great the difficulties and dangers might become. In 1949, first Peking, then Nanking and Shanghai were occupied by the Communist armies.

The China Inland Mission had for many years conducted evangelistic and worship services on its premises in Shanghai (at Woosung Road and later at Sinza Road), both for employees and for others in the area. But soon it became evident that time was running out and David Yang agreed to take over the work and began to build a church out of this ready human material. When missionaries had to leave China and the Mission premises were expected to pass into Communist hands, the trustees of the Free Christian Church, whose European congregation was fast dwindling, decided to hand over the church property to this group of Christians.

David Yang's pastoral experience from 1925 to 1937, his unique experiment with the Spiritual Action Team and his Bible college lecturing provided him with the material for his second book entitled *The Course of the Church*, first published in 1951 but reprinted in Hong Kong in 1962[1]. The present author was privileged to write the Foreword in which, after quoting St. Paul's words in Ephesians 3.9–11, "to make all men see what is the plan of the mystery in the church", he wrote: "Never was there a subject so important for God's children (as that of the Church) and never was there one so misunderstood. History clearly illustrates the fact. Christians are perplexed and uneasy about the subject of the Church because they do not understand the will of God. They recall the Lord's words 'that they might be one' but observe that among God's children there are many dividing walls. So what path is the Church to follow?"

The Church in China had now reached an

[1] Earlier, Pastor Yang had published a commentary on the Letters to the Seven Churches, entitled *Victory and Reward*.

unprecedented crisis. Those Western missionaries who had laid the foundation of the Church and by their knowledge and experience had helped it to grow were about to leave China, so what would the future bring? Some Christians knew little about church teaching and overlooked its importance. On the other hand there were those who went to the opposite extreme. In emphasizing truths about the church they went beyond the Scriptures to the point of "teaching as doctrine the commandments of men". David Yang in his book clearly set forth the true nature of the Church and the ground of its unity. The contents were more positive and less controversial than in Watchman Nee's sensational book *Concerning Our Missions*, later re-titled *The Normal Christian Life*.

8 *Into the Shadows*

One by one David's missionary friends said goodbye as they obtained permits to leave Shanghai for the last time and proceeded to Hong Kong. Chinese Christians, especially the leaders, felt a sense of foreboding about the future, in spite of the fact that the new National Constitution drawn up by the People's Government promised them freedom of belief. Indeed, the representative leaders of the Church had recently been received in Peking by the Premier, Mr. Chou En-lai, and had been given strong reassurances that if they could rid themselves of all "imperialist influences"—meaning the missionaries—and if they were to support government social policies the Church need have nothing to fear.

The Religious Affairs Bureau was set up to handle all China's religions, with a different approach for each. The Protestants adopted the old missionary slogan, "Self-supporting, self-governing, self-propagating", to indicate a complete severance of the Chinese Church from all Western, and particularly American, control and support. What the twenty-five-year-old missionary slogan had not fully succeeded in achieving, in the case of many sections of the church, the People's Government of China achieved at a stroke. The new official united Protestant Church body was called the "Three-Self Patriotic Movement" and such was the pressure to unite under this banner that no church group was in the end able to remain outside, though some at first attempted to do so.

Meanwhile, even as the missionaries were leaving China the Christian "accusation movement" swept the country. Jesus' accusation of the Pharisees for their hypocrisy and evil deeds was regarded as sufficient precedent. Every local church was ordered to call its members together and, under the leadership of a government-appointed cadre, church members were required to rake up the past and to accuse their pastors of actions or attitudes which might be interpreted as favouring foreign imperialism or profiting from it, or of indulging in evil conduct inconsistent with the Christian faith. The pastors could only bow to the criticism and accept the penalties determined by their congregations. Communist cadres skilfully stage-managed the whole process and it was only when this cathartic process was completed that any church was held to be

purged and re-born and so qualified to join the new
united church.

David Yang faced his public trial in his old church
in Nanking. Even a colleague from the China Bible
Seminary, regarded as a very spiritually-minded
Christian, joined in accusing her pastor and senior
lecturer. Great synthetic fervour always attended
these meetings which, for the victims, were harrowing
and utterly humiliating. The result of Pastor Yang's
trial was his ejection from the pastorate of the
Nanking Church on the grounds of being reactionary
in thought, of having been under the influence of
imperialism and of being anti-government. He did
not return to Nanking but concentrated on the
opportunities in Shanghai.

"In my work amongst students," says David
Adeney, "I especially valued his counsels and prayer
fellowship. In a real way he was an elder brother to
me. He also shared with me his perplexity when the
Communists required him to broadcast a criticism
of missionaries on radio. I saw the agony he went
through while writing and re-writing his script. He
well knew that if he refused to co-operate he would
be arrested and imprisoned, not on account of his
faith but on a political charge of collaborating with
the imperialists. I often attended his church in
Shanghai during the fifteen months I spent under
the Communist regime and found fellowship with
him a tremendous source of strength. He himself was
going through great heart-searching as pressure was
put upon him to work with the Three-Self Movement. Some criticized him for compromise but I
knew that he was constantly facing up to the question
of whether it was right for him to work with the
Three-Self Movement and at the same time to be

available to bring encouragement and strength to the Christians, or whether he should refuse and so be deprived of his pastoral ministry. Things became increasingly difficult. He was recognized as an evangelical leader and undoubtedly the authorities used him to draw other evangelicals into the Three-Self Movement by making him a leader in the movement."

When in 1954 a deputation of western clergy from Australia, including Archbishop Mowll, visited China they were presented with a tastefully produced set of photos of the officials of the Three-Self Movement engaged in a variety of activities. David Yang and Marcus Cheng were among them. Realizing that they had overstepped themselves in Nanking and wanting to make some amends to David Yang, the Three-Self organization in 1958 appointed him the Assistant Secretary of the Shanghai Three-Self Committee. However, due to his open loyalty to old evangelical friends, like Dr. Chia Yu-ming and Wang Ming-dao, he came under criticism from Bishop K. T. Ting for being "a two-faced progressive". He was even accused of attempting to revive the ill-famed China Inland Mission! By way of punishment he spent some time being "reformed by labour" and this affected his health.

After that date little was heard of God's servant. Besides teaching at Dr. Chia Yu-ming's Bible School he continued his ministry at the former Free Christian Church for a while but found the strain almost too great to bear. At times he would come to his students after long hours of indoctrination and government discussion meetings only to confess that he had had no time to prepare his lectures. Some of the young people in his church criticized him for compromise. It was easy to say that he had made a mistake but anyone who knew David Yang knew full well that his sole motive was always to serve his Lord and to stand with those who were being tested in their faith. He was convinced that he had a responsibility to continue to minister the Word of God. Eventually he was again accused by the government of "leaning to one side", that is, giving public support to the Three-Self Movement while not really believing in it himself. His opportunity to preach the gospel was taken away and his last years in Shanghai were spent in retirement.

In 1966, during the Cultural Revolution, the Red Guards closed all churches throughout China and humiliated their ministers. These youthful revolutionaries had been charged with the task of eliminating old and out-worn cultures, especially religion, and changing the attitudes and behaviour of the past, both among Party members and the general population. The operations of the Three-Self Patriotic Movement were suspended, although apparently this organization was not struck off the official list of national organizations. Room was left for its possible resuscitation at some future date.

Presumably, the church leaders who were not sent to prison or to labour camps joined the common people in some form or other of productive labour. David Yang must have been among them. But in 1971 a Hong Kong report indicated that in his old age Pastor Yang had returned to his ancestral home in Quwo, Shansi, and from there gone to be with Christ. As late as 1962 a Chinese visitor to Shansi had written, "It is impossible to describe all that I have seen, in a short letter. But God's work is still going on gloriously in the lives of many faithful

Christians. We must join praise and thanks to God for His gracious care and protection. In the past the Church was built upon sand and now it is being built on rock—the Rock. God does not make mistakes. I have been thankful to find brethren steadfast in their faith. This was seen particularly in many young people."

Did David Yang perhaps end his days among his own people rejoicing in the harvest of his earlier labours in south Shansi?

PART 2

NEE DUO-SHENG

Man of Insight

1 *Back to Jerusalem*

Peking, after a short siege, fell to the Communist armies in the freezing early months of 1949, just before the Chinese New Year. The resistance of the demoralized Nationalist forces collapsed as the victorious Red armies swept south. By mid-March they were massing north of the Yangtze River and demanding peace talks. H.M.S. *Amethyst* made its heroic dash down river to Shanghai under Communist guns as Red armies established their bridge-head on the south bank.

"Nanking falls to Red Armies", the big banner headlines announced on April 23rd. The fall of Soochow followed amid growing alarm. Hangchow was occupied on May 5th. City after city south of the Yangtze was falling. By May 17th the battle for Shanghai was joined. On May 25th the great port city was firmly in Communist hands. On October 1st Chairman Mao Tse-tung from the Gate of Heavenly Peace in Peking declared the establishment of the People's Republic of China.

A dilemma was facing Mr. Watchman Nee of Shanghai. He had been on a quick late summer visit to Taiwan to consolidate the work of the "Little Flock" started there in 1947 by refugees from the mainland and to appoint Li Chang-shou (Witness Lee) as leader of the work on the island. Returning to Hong Kong, Mr. Nee found a telegram from Shanghai awaiting him. It reported "Difficulties

within and without. Urge immediate return." But
almost simultaneously Mr. Nee received news of his
mother's death in Foochow (Fuzhou). What was he
to do? Where did his duty and the will of God lie?

"Surely you can't think of returning to Shanghai!
You can be far more useful to the Lord, now, outside
China and you know what is likely to happen to all
Christian leaders in China under the Communists.
In any case, you should attend your mother's
funeral!"

Watchman Nee took time to think and to pray
over this fateful decision.

"Well, what have you decided?"

"To go back to Shanghai! That is where my
responsibilities lie—to my people in Shanghai. You
know our proverb 'Although the wall is about to
collapse I must try to prop it up with my head'. In
any case I know that God is in control. 'The Lord
sits enthroned over the flood: yea, the Lord sits
enthroned as King for ever'. Psalm 29.10."

And like the apostle Paul at Caesarea where his
friends begged him not to go on to Jerusalem because
imprisonment awaited him there, Watchman Nee
might well have echoed: ". . . I am ready not only
to be imprisoned but even to die at Jerusalem for the
name of the Lord Jesus".

As he reached Shanghai, some of his colleagues
were about to make their escape. Saddened,
Watchman Nee determined to redeem the time. On
February 19th, 1950, three hundred people accepted
Christ at evangelistic meetings in the Little Flock
chapel. On July 7th Mr. Nee gave an address on
"Buying up the opportunity". (In Chinese, "crisis"
is represented by two characters meaning "dangerous
opportunity".) For a time the activities in connection

with the assembly continued with increased momentum. Then in April 1951, as foreign missionaries were beginning to stream out of China, the "accusation campaign" burst on the Church. Widespread arrests of so-called counter-revolutionaries and public mass executions were already taking place. The whole country was in the grip of fear. Suicides were a daily event.

The "accusation campaign" was carefully and cunningly planned. Clergy, ministers and leading churchmen were put on trial by their own congregations. Witnesses were thoroughly briefed and every possible criticism on political, moral or ecclesiastical grounds was hurled at the victims, often by their closest friends and colleagues. Watchman Nee did not escape. In 1952, with other Christian leaders all over China, he was arrested and on April 10th a Communist judge sentenced him to twenty years' imprisonment.

Who was this man, to receive such a severe sentence? Why were the Communists so determined to put him out of the way? What had they to fear from him?

2 *The Shadow of Foreign Imperialism*

From the thirteenth century on, Roman Catholic missionaries made spasmodic and largely unsuccessful attempts to introduce Christianity into China. The Jesuits in the seventeenth century achieved some success but were finally expelled in 1722. A handful of French Dominicans lingered on after this event to serve the Catholics scattered all over China, but China had become virtually a closed land to foreigners of any breed.

In 1807 Robert Morrison reached Macao, the Portuguese colony at the mouth of the Pearl River, with a commission from the London Missionary Society to proclaim the gospel to the Chinese. In order to gain occasional access to Canton he accepted a post as interpreter with the East India Company, but his official duties done he devoted all his spare time to the translation of the Bible into Chinese. The Bible was completed in 1819 and Morrison died and was buried in Macao in 1834. But the permission for foreigners to reside on Chinese soil was still denied despite the efforts of Lord Macartney, the British envoy to the Chinese Emperor in Peking.

Numerous Chinese communities in Malaya and the Dutch East Indies had already attracted missionaries who were waiting for the doors of China itself to open. The L.M.S. had a station in Malacca where they set up a school and a printing press.

Meanwhile unofficial trade between India and China was growing. Individual Chinese and foreign traders were making fortunes by trafficking in opium. And it was the burning of a large consignment of British opium in Canton by the Chinese authorities that sparked off the Opium War in 1839. Predictably, it ended in a defeat for the Chinese and the signing of the Treaty of Nanking in 1842. This treaty required China to surrender the island of Hong Kong to the British and to permit foreigners to reside for the purpose of trade and other lawful activities in five ports along the China coast. In these ports foreigners would enjoy extra-territorial rights:

that is, they could be tried for criminal offences only by courts composed of people of their own nationality and not by the Chinese courts of law. This treaty was a shocking humiliation for a proud nation, but worse was to follow. A second war in 1858 led to the sacking of Peking by European troops and was concluded by the Treaty of Peking in 1860. This treaty exacted further territorial concessions on the mainland opposite Hong Kong and additional treaty ports along the coast and up the River Yangtze. Furthermore the opium trade was to be legalized and foreigners allowed freedom of travel everywhere in China. These treaties, ever since known by the Chinese as the "unequal treaties", are still execrated as acts of imperialist aggression against China.

The five original treaty ports were Canton, Amoy, Foochow, Ningpo and Shanghai. Among the first foreigners to move in with the merchants were the waiting missionaries from the U.S.A. and from Great Britain, who, understandably, and unlike the Chinese, saw in the treaties the hand of God in opening the great land of China to the gospel. The treaty ports soon became hives of missionary activity. Consequently the earliest and so the oldest churches in China were established in these five port cities. But the association of the "unequal treaties" and "foreign aggression" with the arrival of the first missionaries meant that Christian missions from the first bore the inescapable stigma of being the tools of imperialism—the spearhead of cultural aggression against China. To this day, foreign missions have never succeeded in living down this reputation and, more unfortunate still, the Chinese Church has had to share this stigma.

D

There had been a Catholic church in Foochow since 1655, but it was not until 1847 that the first Protestants arrived—Mr. Stephen Johnson of the American Board Mission (Congregational) and two couples belonging to the American Methodists. One of the earliest Congregational converts, who became their first ordained minister, was a member of the family of Nee. And so his son, Nee Han-xu, born in 1877, was among the first Chinese children to enjoy a Christian upbringing. In marrying a lady of the house of Lin from the neighbouring province of Kwangtung, he broke with ancient Foochow tradition. Though his wife also came from a Christian home, she was not converted and was, in fact, a revolutionary agitator of a very different temperament from her husband. Mr. Nee held a remunerative post in the Swatow Customs Service. He was a humble, quiet and approachable man, much loved by the younger generation and never known to get angry, while his wife was strict and distant with her family. Their first two children were daughters born in 1900 and 1901. Then on November 4th, 1903, the greatest imaginable "happiness" in Chinese eyes took place—the birth of a first son. His given name was Shu-zu. Later in life he assumed the name of Duo-sheng, meaning the "sound of a bell" and hence, in English, "Watchman". This answer to the parents' prayer moved them to dedicate the child to God's service. Altogether they brought up ten children.

In course of time the Nee family moved back from Swatow (Shantou) to the ancestral home in Foochow. Travelling by coaster they entered the Min River at Pagoda Point and sailed fifteen miles up a cliff-bound gorge to reach Foochow, the provincial capital, lying at the heart of a wide, mountain-encircled and very fertile valley. The Bridge of Ten Thousand Ages links the two banks of the river. European merchants built their homes and offices on the south bank in the suburb of Nantai. The walled city is sited on the north bank and is dominated by the Black Stone Hill with its temples and pleasure grounds. Foochow is known to the Chinese as the "banyan city" on account of the many trees of that variety growing in the town. The city itself appeared drab to the early missionaries, but the surrounding plain, intersected by canals and studded with rural villages, temples and fish-ponds and richly cultivated fields, afforded a beautiful prospect. Timber and tea are the staples of Foochow commerce.

The province of Fukien is separated from the inland provinces by mountains that rise to six or seven thousand feet above sea level, famed for their magnificent scenery. The inhabitants of Fukien have a reputation for being as rugged in character as their surroundings—rough and vigorous, turbulent and industrious. There was something of this in Watchman Nee's make-up.

Three years after the American mission groups had started work in Foochow, the British Church Missionary Society opened a station there in 1850. In 1864 anti-foreign mobs destroyed two of the missions, but the following year the Methodists opened an Anglo-Chinese college. The C.M.S. added Trinity College in 1878, a school including primary, secondary and a divinity section. In the same year mobs again attacked their buildings. Before the end of the century a mission hospital had been opened (the second Chinese lady ever to study medicine abroad was a native of Foochow) and a boarding school, or college. A medical school was established

in 1910, and in 1912 a Union Bible School and a
Normal School for training teachers were opened.
So, at the time of the Revolution in 1911, Foochow
had become an important centre for many forms of
Christian activity.

3   *The School of Obedience*

As a child Shu-zu showed exceptional intelligence
and was looked up to by all the other brothers and
sisters. He was full of ideas for games to play, but also
full of mischief. This got him into frequent trouble
with his austere mother and caused him many a
beating. The home was comfortable and orderly.
Mr. Nee employed a scholar to give the children a
traditional education based on the Confucian
classics. They were divided into classes and Shu-zu
eventually reached a high standard in the composition of essays in the classical style. He was eight years
old when the nationalist revolution of 1911 overthrew
the Manchu dynasty and must have noted his
mother's enthusiastic approval of the event. Once
his classical foundation had been well laid, Shu-zu
went to Trinity College on Black Stone Hill. There
he always came top of his form.

Late in 1919 Miss Dora Yu, a medical student who
became an evangelist, visited Foochow to conduct
a mission at the Congregational Church. Mrs. Nee
attended the meetings but Shu-zu, resentful over an
unjust beating, at first refused to go with the rest of
the family. Though a nominal Christian, Mrs. Nee

had never so far had a personal experience of Christ and it was now, through Miss Yu's ministry that, for the first time, she came into an assurance of salvation. One of the first things she did was to apologize to her son for the false accusation and wrongful punishment. This so impressed the boy that he decided to go and hear Miss Yu preach. The result was that he too entered into the experience of salvation. Miss Dora Yu's campaign initiated a time of renewal for the Foochow Congregational Church.

For Shu-zu new life was accompanied by deep conviction of sin. In particular he felt guilty of the sin of cheating in a Scripture exam. Scripture had been his weakest subject and because of his pride in always being top in everything he had resorted to taking answers into the examination room hidden in the wide sleeve of his Chinese gown. Now he had a troubled conscience about this dishonesty. Expulsion from school was the known penalty for cheating in exams and so he realized that to confess his misdemeanour would probably put an end to all his hopes of a future college career. Nevertheless, Nee knew that he must, at any cost, put the matter right by confessing his sin. In the event, the missionary headmaster, a deeply committed Christian, did not inflict the penalty of expulsion and though Shu-zu never actually went to university this act of obedience and self-humiliation was a turning point in his life and profoundly influenced his future ministry.

Not long after his conversion, Shu-zu met another missionary who was to have a deep influence on his life, Miss Margaret E. Barber. Miss Barber, an independent and dominating character, originally went to China under the Church Missionary Society to teach in the Foochow Anglican Girls School but

when she returned to Foochow in 1920 for a second
term of missionary service, after being baptized by
Mr. D. M. Panton of Surrey Chapel, Norwich, it was
as an independent worker with her friend Miss L. S.
Ballard. The two ladies at first engaged in country
evangelism, but in the stormy post-World War I
years, the conviction grew in their hearts that the
future of the Chinese Church depended on the
emergence of young Chinese leadership.

In the winter of 1921 Miss Dora Yu again visited
Foochow to hold a series of meetings and a remarkable work of grace was seen in the calling out of a
group of young Chinese, all of whom were to make
their mark on the Chinese Church. After these
meetings and because of trouble in his school, young
Nee decided to attend Miss Yu's Bible School in
Shanghai for a year. He then returned to Trinity to
catch up with his studies.

Meanwhile, a young naval officer by the name of
Wang Zai—now better known as Dr. Leland Wang
—and a native of Foochow had gone ashore from his
ship during Miss Yu's second series of meetings. He
had already been converted when his ship had
visited Nanking. Now, hearing singing in a building
as he was passing, his curiosity was aroused, and he
was soon enjoying fellowship with the new converts.
Not long afterwards he resigned his commission in
the navy and returned to Foochow to join the other
young Christians there. His younger brother Wang
Si (Wilson) was a fellow student with Nee at Trinity.
Leland Wang, who was some five years older than
Nee, was soon accepted as their leader, and in 1922
he and Watchman Nee held their first informal
meeting for the "breaking of bread" in Leland
Wang's home—later to be joined by Wilson Wang,

Faithful Luke (one of the new converts) and another
ex-naval officer. Nee, now dissatisfied with the
formality, as he saw it, of the religious life at Trinity,
found in these unstructured gatherings, at which all
were encouraged to participate, something very
appealing. This insignificant little group was in fact
the original assembly of the Little Flock. Mrs. Nee
and two of her sons, including Shu-zu, were baptized
in the river at Pagoda Anchorage in 1922. Faithful
Luke and four others followed their example in the
summer of 1923 and before the end of that year
eighteen more—mostly students—had been baptized.

4 *Learning to Serve*

Nee Shu-zu, John Wang and others worked together
under Leland Wang's leadership for three years or so.
They were quite an independent group and very
original in that they adopted for the first time the
wearing of "gospel shirts"—white cotton jackets with
short Bible texts in large Chinese characters on the
front and back: e.g. "Repent and believe the
gospel", "God so loved the world", "The Kingdom
of Heaven is at hand", etc. Years later these "gospel
shirts" were to become a familiar sight in some circles
outside Mr. Nee's own organization. Beating drums
and singing hymns to attract attention, they then
preached from posters to all who would stop to listen.
Later they used to hold their meetings in homes or
rented halls. Their enthusiasm knew no bounds—
though Nee later looked back with some suspicion

and disapproval on this "carnal" zeal. But they had the joy of leading some to faith in Christ.

In 1925, with the approval and perhaps the sponsorship of Leland Wang, the eventual founder of the Chinese Overseas Mission to the Dutch East Indies (Indonesia), Nee Shu-zu accompanied his mother on a journey to Sitiawan in Malaya where the Methodist Church had invited her to hold evangelistic meetings. She was a forceful speaker. The mission was not a great success, numerically speaking, as the local Chinese were preoccupied with rubber tapping. But the formation of a small assembly by the converts resulted.

On their return to Foochow, differences of opinion arose between Watchman Nee and Leland Wang over what Nee called the "purity of the testimony" and interpretations of Scripture. Finally Nee was put out of the fellowship with the Foochow assembly and not invited to take part in the New Year convention.

Meanwhile Miss Barber, in 1923, had hired a disused twenty-room factory at Pagoda, the anchorage port at the mouth of the Min River, some ten miles from Foochow, and was holding regular Bible classes there for the young people. She had no close contact with the Foochow assembly. So when Nee parted company with Leland Wang, he went to join Miss Barber. Her instruction in the deeper aspects of the Christian life, the work of the Holy Spirit and the walk of faith left a lasting impression on him. For Nee they were formative years and the teaching received was greatly to affect his future ministry. Miss Barber became his confidante and adviser. She directed his reading and introduced him to the writings of Samuel Govett and D. M. Panton—two men who, significantly enough, had resigned from the Anglican ministry. She also introduced him to the works of Mrs. Jessie Penn-Lewis, Dr. Andrew Murray, the saintly South African, and, not least, J. N. Darby and the early Brethren. In the latter he recognized "a simpler, more flexible pattern of church fellowship". Nee did not always see eye to eye with Miss Barber, particularly in the matter of women's ministry, but she on her part dealt faithfully with her young friend. Miss Barber possessed a poetic gift and some of her hymns later found their way into the collection which Mr. Nee published for the use of the Shanghai Church. Miss Barber's fruitful life came to an end in 1930, but Miss Ballard, with a Chinese fellow worker, was still living and working in Foochow in 1948 when China was about to fall to the Communists.

From a simple hut halfway between Foochow and Pagoda Point where he took up residence in 1925, the young budding evangelist accepted invitations to C.M.S. churches in the province and to the Presbyterians in Amoy. In between journeys he read widely and studied. He also paid visits to Shanghai and Nanking where he was gratified to meet people who had read and appreciated *Revival*, a magazine which he had begun to publish in 1923 while he was still at school and only twenty years of age.

It was in Shanghai that Nee, at twenty-five, began to write his first book, *The Spiritual Man*. Like Mrs. Penn-Lewis, Nee based his writing on the assumption that man's nature is tripartite—body, soul and spirit—a Greek rather than a Hebrew concept. "The Hebrews stressed the duality of man in terms of soul and spirit. These were always a unit and it was impossible for a Hebrew to talk about man's spirit as if it were an independent element" (Fred Wagner in *HIS* magazine, January 1973). Nee therefore analysed all religious experience as being either physical (emotional), psychical or spiritual. During the writing of the book he became very ill with tuberculosis and feared he was going to die. Returning to Foochow in 1926, he continued his work, completing Volume I the following year. The remaining two volumes were completed later in Shanghai.

In 1927 Nee had a fresh spiritual experience. He describes it in these words: "For some years after my conversion I had been taught to 'reckon'. I 'reckoned' from 1920 until 1927. The more I 'reckoned' that I was dead to sin, the more alive I clearly was. I simply could not believe myself dead and I could not produce the death. Whenever I sought help from others I was told to read Romans 6.11 and the more I read that verse and tried to 'reckon', the further away death was. I could not get at it. . . . For months I was seeking and at times fasted, but nothing came through. I remember one morning—one I can never forget—I was upstairs sitting at my desk reading the Word and praying and I said, 'Lord, open my eyes!' And then in a flash I saw it. I saw my oneness with Christ. I saw that I was in Him and that when He died, I died. I saw that the question of my death was a matter of the past and not of the future and that I was just as truly dead as He was because I was in Him when He died. The whole thing had dawned upon me. I was carried away with such joy at this great discovery that I jumped from my chair and shouted, 'Praise the Lord, I am dead!'. . . . From that day to this I have never for one moment doubted the finality of that word 'I have been crucified with Christ'." (*The Normal Christian Life.*)

The Reverend Calvin Chao once expressed the opinion that only a third generation Christian can, from experience, expound the Scriptures with the depth of understanding of an Andrew Murray or a Bishop Handley Moule. First generation Christians find it hard to escape the taint of their pagan heredity and background. Even a second generation Christian may still lack deep spiritual apprehension. Watchman Nee was a third generation Christian who, in many respects, attained to a unique Christian maturity. He had a penetrating insight into Divine truth and a rare ability to unfold the mysteries of God's Word. This he did with eloquence and charm, for his was a personality possessed of God, and a heart and mind deeply taught of the Spirit. Here was a man raised up to be a leader in the hour of China's need and a teacher for the world of the deep things of God.

5 *Independency and Nationalism*

It was in 1928 that Mr. Nee's life work really began, for in that year "Watchman" Nee, as he had begun to call himself, moved permanently to Shanghai, the most Western city in China and a hot-bed of anti-foreign agitation which flared into violence in 1926. In Shanghai, Mr. Nee made no attempt to associate with any existing church but very soon established his own congregation in Hardoon Road in the

British Settlement. Many of its early members were students.

That Mr. Nee held a poor view of the churches of his time can be seen from an "Open Letter" which he published in 1928 in *Revival*:

"God's purpose for today is speedily to complete the body of His Son and to destroy His enemies and bring in the Kingdom. But we may also say that God's purpose in this generation is actually being hindered by the church. We firmly believe that before long God is going to gather together all His children into one so that His church will not merely cease to be a hindrance but will work with God to complete His eternal purpose. We humbly hope that in the hands of God we may have a small share in this glorious work.

"The darkness of this present generation is clearly recognized by those who have eyes to see. What we witness today is almost entirely the works of man. Yes, of the many admirable activities which people tend to regard as spiritual, how many really are the works of God? Most pitiable of all, much work 'for the Lord' or 'for the sake of God's people' is no more than the effects of the corrupt flesh of man. Men have not sought God's will nor listened to God's command nor trusted in the power of God in their work. God's children have acted largely according to what they thought best. Today we have everything—except God: human thoughts and man-made plans and human endeavour are all put in the place of God. If God's children do not repent they will find that they have no spiritual usefulness; that they have missed the work of God and suffered loss themselves."

Referring to the new congregations in Foochow and Shanghai, Mr. Nee, then only twenty-six years of age, wrote: "This new witness that has been raised up will undoubtedly arouse misunderstanding, but what comforts me is that those who really want to live entirely in accordance with the Lord's truth will know real freedom in our midst."

The threat was immediately recognized by other evangelical groups in both cities. "Both in Shanghai and in Foochow, Christian schools and colleges vainly forbade students to attend the meetings."[1] And the new movement gradually began to attract some of the best and most spiritually minded Christians away from their own churches. Entire congregations, especially in the province of Chekiang, in some cases broke away from their own parent associations in search of this promised "freedom" of which Mr. Watchman Nee preached and wrote. The China Inland Mission work was hard hit.

In laying emphasis on the autonomy of the local congregation Mr. Nee was not contributing anything new to the historic arguments. Many of his convictions on this subject are shared by every branch of the Christian Brethren, by Congregationalists (his father's denomination) and by Baptists. He advocated the Acts pattern of initially setting up home churches which were to be self-supporting from the start. Only as the congregation matured and developed their own leadership did he allow the question of simple places of worship to be considered. This was certainly in contrast to the practice of many missionary societies which tended to lay undue emphasis on elaborate church buildings and on schools, and undertook, initially at least, to pay the salaries of pastors, evangelists and caretakers. Under these circumstances, eventual "self-support" became a

[1] Hollington T'ong: *Christianity in Taiwan—a History.*

frightening prospect for poor Christian communities. Not all missions in China, however, were following this method. Some had always laid emphasis on the autonomy of the local church and did so increasingly after the traumatic events of 1926 when missionaries were evacuated from inland China in the face of anti-foreign and anti-Christian agitation stirred up by the growing Communist movement.

What Watchman Nee's critics found most difficult to accept was his contention that there can be only one church in each geographical locality and that every church which exists on any other than geographical grounds is not a true church. By implication only the churches which Nee founded were true churches and all others were on unscriptural grounds.

But were there other subconscious reasons for Nee's independency? Undoubtedly, yes. Communist agitators had been denouncing Chinese Christians in the employ of foreign missions as "running dogs of the Imperialists" and re-emphasizing the old myth that foreign missionaries were part and parcel of the foreign imperialist aggression against China. Such insults and accusations were extremely embarrassing for all Chinese Christians and especially for the leaders in the mainline Chinese denominations. Even the adoption of mission policies to promote the autonomy of Chinese churches was not enough for many Chinese Christians, who saw their only hope for the future in terms of total independence from foreign organizations and from missionary control. As a result, several significant independent movements came to birth.

As early as 1917 in Peking, a group known as the "True Jesus Church" had been founded by Chang Lin-shen. Then in 1921 Ching Tien-ying had founded the "Jesus Family" in Shantung. Finally, in 1928, the Little Flock was launched in Shanghai by Nee Duo-sheng. As with the other movements, it was the combination of old Biblical principles and the new ardent nationalism which influenced Watchman Nee to develop his independent policies. Pragmatic motives and the spirit of Chinese nationalism, in other words, as much as doctrinal distinctiveness without question lay behind all these movements. Consciously or subconsciously they were an attempt to escape the stigma of association with "western missionary imperialism". Criticism of western missions centred on their Anglo-American traditions and practices, their inaccurate translations and interpretations of the Scriptures and the inability of the western missionary to fit into Chinese culture or to identify himself with the community. In the light of the apostle Paul's teaching about the supranational character of the Church, it would not be wrong to call such nationalism a sin, though it has seldom been recognized as such.

But the independent church is a phenomenon not unique to China. In Japan the "Mukyokai" or "No-church" movement had, by 1962, attracted an estimated 50,000 to 75,000 members into their fellowship. In Brazil, the independent "Congregations of Christ in Brazil", founded in 1910, numbered 265,000 in 1962 and are still growing rapidly. David Barrett's *Schism and Renewal in Africa* claims 6,000 independent churches for that continent with a total membership of millions. There are corresponding movements in every continent. In Taiwan today, one-third of all Protestant Christians are in the independent churches. The reaction against western missions, as distinct from Christianity, has been worldwide.

The "Little Flock" derived its name from the fact that Watchman Nee's first collection of hymns published in 1928 was entitled *The Hymns for the Little Flock* (cf. Luke 12.32, "Fear not, little flock; for it is your Father's good pleasure to give you the kingdom"). While outsiders forthwith dubbed the movement the "Little Flock", Watchman Nee's own preferred designation for each local church was, for example, "Foochow Local Gathering of Believers in the Lord's Name" or, simply, at a later stage, "The Foochow Christian Meeting Place" and later still "The Foochow Church". From the establishment of the first church in Foochow in 1923 until 1949 more than 700 such churches with a membership of 70,000 were established. Some were taken over from the missionary organizations but others never had any connection with western missions. All were entirely under the leadership of Chinese nationals and, of course, financially independent. In 1938 Watchman Nee published *Concerning Our Missions* which set out his main position in the interpretation of the Church. It was in fact a series of lectures to his fellow-workers and an updated version of a previous publication, *The Life of the Assembly*. The editor of later editions of this work re-titled it *The Normal Christian Church Life* to match other titles in the series. Mr. Nee's main contentions on the subject of the Church are as follows:

1. Denominationalism is a sin, a degenerate form of organization. This claim is based on an interpretation of Galatians 5.20 in which "heresies", one of the "works of the flesh", should, according to Nee, be translated "denominations". It follows that if denominations are sinful, they must be the enemy of the spiritual man. Therefore all believers ought to

come out of such unclean organizations and encourage other believers to follow them.

2. Since all churches in the New Testament are identified only by the name of a particular geographical locality, churches patterned on the New Testament can only exist on the basis of locality, independent from all other such local churches and completely autonomous as to government and finance: "one church, one locality". No other form of church government can be justified from Scripture.

3. Because present-day churches have departed from the principles laid down in Scripture, true Christians must repent and should endeavour to set up local churches on Biblical and apostolic principles. Churches must stand on the ground of undenominational local churches, meeting solely "in the Lord's Name".

The book, published in Chinese and later in English, was a bombshell! It was immediately recognized as an open attack, a declaration of war, both on denominational foreign missions and also on interdenominational missions. New separatist local churches were being set up in many of the larger cities claiming to be the only ones with Biblical justification. It would be untrue to say that this separatist movement did not cause intense resentment on the part of many of the older churches and not a little bitterness on the part of those who saw the fruit of their life-work being taken over by another organization. On the positive side, many old denominational churches were aroused from their sleep by the Nee challenge to realize how useless in themselves were the traditional customs and forms of worship practised in many congregations. However, the "one church, one locality" principle so

E

firmly held, led to a denial of all other churches as
not real churches at all and the required total
breaking of fellowship with them was divisive. In
condemning denominationalism as such the "Little
Flock" itself became a sect in the sense of St. Paul's
condemnation of those in Corinth who claimed to be
"of Christ" (1 Cor. 1.12). Pastor David Yang's book
The Course of the Church, based on a totally different
background experience, covered much the same
ground as *Concerning Our Missions* but lacked the
divisive and schismatic tendencies of Watchman
Nee's work and rejected his more extreme and
narrow views.

6 *Nee-style Revival*

Mr. Nee laid a greatly needed stress on the building
up of believers in truth and experience so that they
in turn could take their share of responsibility in all
departments of church life. Many churches had
become content with a spiritually shallow experience
and a quite inadequate instruction in the truths of
the Word of God. Their members were therefore,
for the most part, incapable of taking their share in
church life and were content to leave everything to
the paid minister. Canon David Paton comments:
"The result of professional clericalism exported to
the mission field at all events is evident—it is
sterility."[1] Church growth, Nee emphasized, is not
just the result of hard work but requires true spiritual

[1] *Christian Missions and the Judgment of God* by David N. Paton.

life beginning in a spiritual birth. Only that which has spiritual life can grow spiritually and reproduce itself. This had been a neglected truth until God raised up a number of His servants in the 1920's to give it a new prominence.

Reference has already been made to *Revival*, the magazine which made its first appearance in Foochow in 1923 when Mr. Nee was still at school. It continued to be published irregularly whenever the funds were available. The early numbers contained articles like "Preach only the deep mysteries of God", "Preach only the principles of the spiritual life", etc. When, at a later date, people suggested that the contents might be simpler, Mr. Nee replied, "God's Church has a journal which concentrates on spiritual principles, preaching nothing else but the basic laws of the spiritual life, so that those who are really seeking progress in their spiritual life may have a little light on their pathway. . . . We admit that *Revival* is not for all believers, but it is for all believers in need." Issue after issue exposed the superficiality of much current church life, and the inability of some ministers to lead their members on towards spiritual maturity. Consequently, the argument went, the churches remained conformed to the world and unable to take in advanced teaching. Their Christian faith had no solid foundation and so they were weak in resisting sin. Quality was being sacrificed for quantity. New members were being added who were not "born again" and the composition of the congregations was thus becoming more and more confused. In some cases, even basic truth had been abandoned.

So went Mr. Nee's diagnosis of the general church situation in China. It was both true and at the same

time far too sweeping. It implied that few except the
"Little Flock" assemblies were faithfully preaching
and teaching the Word of God and building their
church life on the pattern of God's Word. This was
far from being the case. Nevertheless the emphasis
on the neglected truth of regeneration and the new
life of the Spirit was certainly needed. This teaching
ministry was the revival of which the magazine
testified. It bore little resemblance to traditional
"revival meetings" like those being held all over
China at that time by both missionary and Chinese
"revivalists". The publication of *Revival* gradually
gained nation-wide acceptance because it responded
to a deep need wherever Christians were being
spiritually starved. Circulating throughout the
country, it had the effect of bringing Mr. Nee's
teaching and his work in Foochow and Shanghai to
the attention of Christians everywhere.

In 1931, Mr. Nee invited a number of Chinese
leaders, including his old friend Leland Wang and
Dr. John Sung, the well-known scholar-evangelist,
and some Western missionary leaders to a conference
in Shanghai. He was hoping to persuade other
Chinese pastors and congregations to follow his own
pattern of church life. But in this he failed. Little
ground for agreement could be found between his
own separatist views and those of his Chinese and
Western guests.

In December 1930 an international group of eight
leaders among the Exclusive Brethren led by Mr.
Charles Barlow had paid a visit to Shanghai and
Foochow to minister to the Little Flock assemblies.
They were deeply impressed with what they saw and
with Watchman Nee himself. So, in 1933, they
invited Mr. Nee to visit England and America.

Arriving, after a restful sea voyage, in England in June, he was warmly entertained by Mr. Barlow at Peterborough, visited a number of the assemblies and took part in at least one conference in Islington. Mr. Nee also slipped away from his hosts to pay an unscheduled visit to the Honor Oak Fellowship and to Mr. Austin-Sparks whose writings he appreciated. He was accompanied to the United States by Mr. James Taylor Snr., the pontifical American Exclusive Brethren leader. Conversations on the ship revealed divergencies of interpretation of the Book of Revelation, but they ministered together in New York. Later, when news reached Taylor that Nee had "broken bread" with his old friend Dr. Thornton Stearns of Cheloo University, Taylor expressed his strong disapproval. In Vancouver Mr. Nee had a brief reunion with another old friend with whom he had enjoyed fellowship in his early days in Shanghai —Mr. Charles Judd of the China Inland Mission.

During Mr. Nee's absence from China, Chefoo in Shantung became the scene of a revival affecting several of the churches—an extension of the revival which was stirring the Southern Baptist Churches in the province and which owed something to the campaigns of the Bethel Worldwide Evangelistic Band under the leadership of Mr. Andrew Gih. In the Chefoo Little Flock assembly where Witness Lee was among the leaders, many gave up all their possessions for the furtherance of the Lord's work. This enabled seventy families to migrate to the north-west as "instant" congregations and bases for evangelism. Thirty other families went to the north-east of China. As a result, by 1944 forty new assemblies had come into existence.

The China Christian Year Book for 1935 for the first

time gave mention to the Little Flock and admitted
that the movement was gaining rapidly in Chekiang
and was drawing away church members and some
leaders from the regular churches.

7 *Marriage and Travel Overseas*

Among Watchman Nee's childhood companions was
a lively, attractive girl whose parents were friends of
his own family. But when Nee was converted Pin Hui
remained a gay, modern lass with no interest in
religion. It was clear that, attractive though she was
to him, he could not then consider her as a wife. His
feelings were at that time expressed in a hymn which
is also included in the Little Flock hymnbook.

> The love of Jesus is wide, deep and high: how can
>   it be measured?
> If it were not so, how could a sinner like me be
>   reached by it?
> My Lord paid the price to redeem me for Himself,
> So I am ready to bear the Cross and faithfully
>   follow Him.
> Now I forsake all in order to gain Christ,
> Whether life or death, yea, nothing will make me
>   turn back.
> Friends, ambitions, gain—of what use are they?
> My gracious Lord became poor for me, so I will
>   become poor for Him.
> I love my Saviour, I plead His faithfulness;
> For His sake, comfort may turn to pain and gain
>   to loss.

Thou art my comfort, my gracious Lord;
What is there in heaven or earth to compare with
   Thee?
Suffering, opposition, pain I regard them not;
I only ask that Thy love be poured into my soul
   and body.
Lord, I plead, give grace to guide your child;
Stand by me and give me strength to pass through
   this dark, sinful world.
Satan, the world, the flesh—all continually tempt
   me;
If you don't give me strength I fear I may bring
   shame on your Name.
The time remaining is short, so save me from the
   world;
And when you come I'll sing Hallelujah, Amen.

After High School days in Foochow, Pin Hui went
to Peking to enter the Christian Yenching University.
There she found the Lord as her Saviour and some
years later moved south again to Shanghai, where
she gravitated to the "Little Flock" assembly at
Hardoon Road. The earlier acquaintance with
Watchman Nee was renewed and this friendship
ripened into a romance and finally marriage in
Hangchow on October 16th, 1934. They had no
children, but having had a literary education,
"Charity" Nee became of great assistance to her
husband in his publication work.

In 1938, Mr. Nee again visited Great Britain and
Europe. He arrived in England in July just in time
to attend the Keswick Convention, where the
Chairman, Rev. W. H. Aldis, invited him to offer a
prayer at one of the meetings in the big tent. A
Japanese Christian happened to be on the same

platform. The war between China and Japan had
already been in progress for just a year—the war
which was eventually to merge with the second world
war two years later. The atrocities committed by the
Japanese during "the rape of Nanking" had horrified
the world. And so the spirit of that prayer, as Mr.
Nee interceded, not only for China, but also for
Japan, deeply moved the great gathering and left an
indelible impression on the minds of many who were
present.

In his search for Christians of like mind with
himself, Watchman Nee renewed his acquaintance
with Mr. Austin-Sparks, a former Baptist minister,
the author of books about the place of the Cross in
Christian experience and the leader of the Honor Oak
Fellowship Centre in south London. There he was
entertained and invited to speak. His teaching on
Romans with its distinction between the Blood and
its efficacy for sins and the Cross with its efficacy for
sin was well received. The Honor Oak teaching on
the Church also closely resembled his own teaching
which had in each case led its followers into ecclesiastical exclusivism.[1] A lasting bond of fellowship was
established between the Little Flock in China and
the Honor Oak Fellowship in London. When news
reached the Exclusive Brethren leaders that Mr. Nee
had "broken bread" at Honor Oak, he was immediately put out of their fellowship.

Before returning to China, Mr. Nee, accompanied
by Miss Elizabeth Fischbacher, formerly of the
China Inland Mission, and Pastor David Yang's
close friend, visited Copenhagen and Paris where

[1] The Honor Oak Fellowship eventually abandoned its
exclusive position and is now a local church welcoming
fellowship with all other evangelical churches.

they began to translate *Concerning Our Missions* for
Mr. Austin-Sparks' opinion. Mr. Nee in fact returned
to England on December 31st, 1938, and remained
in London until May before returning to China.
During this time he met G. H. Lang, the Open
Brethren teacher, and had a long discussion with Mr.
Norman Baker of the China Inland Mission on the
subject of indigenous church policies in China. A
letter written by Mr. Nee to Mr. Baker after studying
"The Principles and Practice of the China Inland
Mission" expressed strong disapproval of the document which, as he understood it, advocated a
mission-imposed autonomy which did not allow the
churches to determine their own pathway. The
controversy between the Missions and the Little
Flock was at its height and Rev. W. H. Aldis, Home
Director of the China Inland Mission, wrote a
gracious farewell letter to Mr. Nee pleading for more
toleration and Christian fellowship among Christians
of like faith in China. But Watchman Nee returned
to Shanghai confirmed in his convictions.

Watchman Nee in China had attracted many
outstanding women followers including several
notable missionaries, but he had few men of stature
to help him. His visit to the West was an almost
pathetic search for fellowship, and the one man not
involved in the missionary enterprise who was able
to enter into his thinking was Mr. Austin-Sparks.

Meanwhile, another interesting figure had appeared on the Indian scene and the ministry of
Bakht Singh and the assemblies which he created
formed a third point in the triangle of similar
ministries in England, China and India.

During the war, the Little Flock, like other
churches, came under strong pressures from the

Japanese occupation authorities to join a United Church. Refusal to conform meant that the gatherings of the central church in Shanghai were forced to discontinue for the duration of the war. But members continued to "break bread" in private homes throughout the city. In North China, apparently, Little Flock assemblies met with little trouble and continued to flourish.

8 *Literary Ventures*

Mr. Nee's addresses and sermons were all recorded in the periodicals *Preaching Notes*, *The Christian* and *Revival*. His first major book, *The Spiritual Man*, published in 1928, was a three-volume work of 1,000 pages. It is an illustration of the ability of Mr. Nee to assimilate the contents of the spiritual classics of the West and to reproduce their essential truths for the benefit of Chinese readers. For instance, his view that only "victorious Christians", or "overcomers", will find a place in the Kingdom was adopted from the writings of Samuel Govett. Teaching about the "partial rapture" of only "overcoming" Christians at the Second Coming was derived from the writings of D. M. Panton of Surrey Chapel, Norwich. He had often discussed this subject with his close friend Charles H. Judd of the China Inland Mission in whose home in Woosung Road he was a constant visitor when he first arrived in Shanghai. *The Spiritual Man*, written when Nee was only twenty-five, borrows heavily from Mrs. Jessie Penn-Lewis' *Body*,

Soul and Spirit and the works of Andrew Murray of South Africa. In a period when revival movements were widespread throughout China, the book served a very useful purpose in warning the Christians against Satanic deceptions and in helping them to discern between the false and the true, between what was genuine and what was spurious revival, between the work of the Holy Spirit and the work of deceiving spirits.

The Spiritual Man was followed by *The Hymns for the Little Flock*—127 translations of foreign classics, original compositions of his own and by Miss Barber and meditations on the Song of Solomon by Miss Ting Xu-Xin. The book soon gained popularity and affection as an outstanding collection of expressions of adoration, devotion and worship.

In the West a series of widely read and warmly praised books have been published under Watchman Nee's name. Actually he only wrote two books for publication—*The Spiritual Man* and *The Normal Christian Church Life* (*Concerning Our Missions*). All other publications under his name in the English language are edited collections of Mr. Nee's sermons and messages given at conferences or to his fellow-workers and extracted from the previously mentioned periodicals and other manuscripts. The best known titles are: *The Normal Christian Life* (1940); *The Normal Christian Worker* (1948); *Changed into His Likeness*; *Sit, Walk, Stand*; *Love Not the World*; *What Shall This Man Do?*; *A Table in the Wilderness*; *The Song of Songs* and *The Release of the Spirit*.

Countless people the world over have been greatly enriched by the spiritual insights contained in Watchman Nee's writings and his emphasis on the place of the Cross in Christian experience. While he himself has languished in a Communist prison, the Word of the Lord through him has not been bound.

What were the "deep mysteries of God" which Watchman Nee taught? They are probably most clearly stated in *The Release of the Spirit*, which bears many resemblances to the teaching of a contemporary missionary in China, Miss Ruth Paxon, who shared Mr. Nee's views as to the tripartite nature of man and wrote *Life on the Highest Plane*. Watchman Nee conceived of man in terms of three concentric circles: the outward man is the body, the outer man is the soul and the inner man—or innermost circle—is the spirit. God's purpose is for the Holy Spirit in union with the human spirit (the inner man) to govern the soul (the outer man) and for both soul and spirit to use the body (the outward man) as their means of expression. But, to ensure this, it is essential for the soul to be "smitten a fatal blow", "destroyed" or "broken" as to its self-strength and self-government, by the Cross. That essential and crucial experience enables the believer to separate and distinguish between what is "soulish" (at the mental level) and what is "spiritual" (at the level of the Holy Spirit). Essential to this experience is a supernatural revelation—the light which unbares and shows up the "soul" or "flesh" for what it is. *The Release of the Spirit* repeats over and over again statements such as "stricken with light", "as soon as the light shines, the flesh is dead", "whatever is revealed in the light is slain by it", "light both reveals and slays", "the Cross means the breaking of the outward man", "the breaking of the outward man is the basic experience of all who serve God", "once the outward man is broken, man's spirit naturally abides in the presence of God without ceasing", "once the natural man is broken, one no longer needs to retreat Godward, for one is always in the presence of God", "this kind of fellowship among Christians is possible only after our outward man is shattered", "the marvellous thing is that after your outward man is destroyed, you can be strong whenever you want to", "the dividing of spirit and soul depends upon enlightenment" and so on.

Teaching of this kind obviously has a strong appeal for the searcher after a deeper union with Christ. But many find some aspects of these "mysteries" to be too mystical. They re-echo the journals of Mme. Guyon with which Nee was familiar and Christian mystics of earlier times. And they tend to encourage a form of spirituality which is introspective and divorced from the harsh realities of life in the real world of today. The teaching of a spiritual crisis called "the death of the soul" also suggests a kind of automatic sanctification akin to "sinless perfection", resulting in an insensitivity to temptation. Not the least danger is the equating of the soul with the mind and the consequent discrediting of the use of the mind in the service of God or the understanding of the Scriptures. This verges on heresy, for our Lord taught His disciples to love God with the mind and soul as well as the heart. Nee himself did not go to this extreme but Witness Lee of Taiwan has definitely strayed on to this ground and in so doing promotes an unbiblical anti-intellectualism. Some who have at first enthusiastically embraced this teaching have subsequently been disappointed and disillusioned with its outworking. In *The Normal Christian Life*, a profound and usually helpful exposition of the Epistle to the Romans, this conception of what it means to be crucified is again present.

Other books encourage the reader to assess all Christian activity in terms of that which is "soulish" and that which is "spiritual". This tends to produce a passivity or quietism because of fear of serving God on the "soulish" level. And, applied to the Church, it leads to a deep suspicion of the many normal expressions of Christian activity as being merely "soulish" and therefore "unspiritual". This in turn leads to criticism and even condemnation of much Christian tradition and a turning inward to a fellowship from which all but the inner circle are excluded. The implication of this teaching was to see the true Church of Jesus Christ as represented only by a small minority in every place—in China by the Little Flock assemblies only—and to dismiss all other expressions of church life as spurious.

The Holy Spirit was, of course, given due prominence in Watchman Nee's preaching as the Giver of special gifts to individuals and to churches. "Tongues", though acceptable and not forbidden, were not allowed to dominate the "exercise of spiritual gifts" meetings. Neither Watchman Nee nor Witness Lee ever spoke in tongues themselves, even during the period when many in the Little Flock were seeking new spiritual experiences.

The preaching of Watchman Nee between 1928 and 1950, and the subsequent publication of his lectures and sermons in print, most certainly reveal a man of deep spirituality. His teaching met a great contemporary need and, in spite of its extremes in certain respects, and its other-worldliness, it was more free from error than that which was current in both the True Jesus Church and the Jesus Family. In the case of the former, their theology of the Trinity seems to have been at fault, particularly in relation to the eternal Sonship of Christ. "Feet washing" was also regarded as an essential sacrament and the failure to practise it meant that one had no part in the Lord, according to a literal reading of Jesus' words in John 13.6–10. The Jesus Family, for its part, has become well known for its practice of communal living—an extended family, having possessions, children and all things in common. Dr. Vaughan Rees' book *The Jesus Family in Communist China* has described this attempt to anticipate Communism on a Christian basis, and the Communists were undoubtedly impressed with what they saw of the experiment. But Dr. Rees does not record the erratic history of the Jesus Family and its origin in extreme Pentecostalism, its emphasis at one period on direct revelation from God through the Holy Spirit by dreams and visions quite independently of the Scriptures, its frequent insistence on mass prayer in preference to individual prayer, its intense emotionalism, its notorious lawsuits to obtain possession of church property not theirs, its spiritual "love-ins", etc. The Jesus Family was forcibly disbanded by the Communists in 1953. Unfortunately the Jesus Family has sometimes been confused with the Little Flock as if they were one and the same thing. Nothing is further from the truth, though in 1950 Mr. Nee was advocating attempts to win over Jesus Family groups to the Little Flock fellowship.

The Little Flock remained true to the Scriptures, even though its leaders sometimes erred in their private interpretations of certain doctrines and went to unscriptural extremes in others as now must be recorded.

9 A Commercial Venture

As Mr. Nee's work gained increasing importance throughout the 1930s problems inevitably multiplied. It was one thing to lay down firm New Testament principles and to insist on the strict autonomy of the local church, but what about "the ministry", a subject under constant debate after 1947 when Little Flock teaching became less inward looking and more outward reaching? The first issue of a bi-monthly magazine of this name appeared in May 1948. Mr. Nee, though critical of the "professional" ministry as practised by the denominations, faced the problem of the support of the growing band of preachers and teachers whom he was training. Were they or were they not members of local churches and who should be responsible for their support?

In *The Normal Christian Church Life* Mr. Nee had discussed this problem: "The Apostle Paul himself, while in Corinth, made tents and did not there depend on the rewards of preaching the gospel (1 Cor. 9). This shows that the servant of the Lord may be supported in two ways: one by working with his own hands for appropriate payment and the other by preaching the gospel while looking to God for divine supply. Those who preach the gospel live by the gospel; they do not ask the brothers and sisters to be responsible for their support, but believe that God will supply. Thus working with our hands is one way and trusting God to supply our needs is another way. There is no third way. For Paul to work with his own hands was good, but in the case of Paul this was exceptional and not normal. Paul, as a servant of God, merely complied with circumstances and is not therefore a pattern for others to follow. Indeed, Paul admits that others are not like him in this respect, as he shows so clearly in 1 Corinthians 9."

In spite of the views Mr. Nee here expressed about the abnormality of Paul's tent-making interludes, he continued to advocate the two possible patterns open to the servant of God in the matter of support—the way of trust in God and the way of self-support. Many Little Flock workers, therefore, did in fact engage in various business or professional pursuits to support themselves.

In about 1940 Mr. Nee's younger brother had started the Sheng Hua Drug Manufacturing Factory in Shanghai. But being a research scientist rather than a business man he did not make a financial success of the venture. So Mr. Nee, both to assist his brother and as a way of "tent-making" for the support of his co-workers, became first a director of the firm and in 1942 the chairman of the board of directors. This action met with the strong disapproval of the elders of the Hardoon Road assembly. Mr. Nee was requested to stop preaching and seldom preached again for about five years. It would appear that for various reasons, not least the hostilities with Japan, the factory was a source of constant worry to the directors. In 1945, the war over, Mr. and Mrs. Nee were on a visit to West China and there met Stephen Chan, Mr. Nee's nephew, in Chungking. To the nephew it was apparent that the factory was weighing heavily on Mr. Nee's mind. Within three

F

days he had to find $10,000,000 to enable the factory to continue production. He was obviously in no mood for social intercourse! Indeed, the strain of these business worries and the breath of scandal in the post-war years brought on another period of ill health. He had become ensnared and entangled in the affairs of the world. To make matters worse, his example had encouraged preachers outside the Little Flock assemblies to supplement their meagre incomes by engaging in business—to their own spiritual loss.

Finally, in 1947, Mr. Nee made a public confession of his error in becoming involved in the business of the factory and "handed over" the factory to the Shanghai local church, following, as he claimed, the precedent in Acts 4. This action had a profound effect on the whole church and, in a wave of enthusiasm, one member after another began to "hand over" their businesses, their investments and their property to the local church. The theme of "handing over" occupied much of Mr. Nee's preaching at the time— as though it was a new discovery of "truth"—"handing over" possessions, "handing over" oneself and "handing over" churches. Great enthusiasm was aroused but equally heated discussion engendered. Wives were often unwilling for husbands to "hand over" all the family possessions. Church elders were divided as to the rightness of handing over their local church to the control of others. Moreover the Shanghai church suddenly became the embarrassed owners of a chemical factory, an ink factory, a printing works, and much property hitherto privately owned. All this was in flat contradiction to the following passage in *The Normal Christian Church Life*:

"The business of the churches consists in the mutual care of their various members, such as with the conduct of meetings for breaking of bread, for the exercise of spiritual gifts, for the study of the Word, for prayer, for fellowship and for gospel preaching. The work is beyond the sphere of any church as a corporate body; it is the responsibility of individuals though not of individuals as such. There is no scriptural precedent for such work being undertaken by a church as, for instance, hospitals or schools or even something on a more spiritual plane such as foreign missions. It is perfectly in order for one or more members of a church to run a hospital or a school, or to be responsible for missionary work, but not for any church as a whole. A church exists for the purpose of mutual help in one place, not for the purpose of bearing the responsibility of work in different places."

Obviously the conduct of factories and secular enterprises now undertaken by the local Shanghai church was a far greater departure from principle than running hospitals and schools! But was it, like the Jesus Family experiment, also an attempt to steal the Communist thunder? The final nemesis came in 1952 when one of the Communist charges against Mr. Nee was that of being a capitalist. The factory enterprise thus proved to be a more serious mistake than Mr. Nee had realized in 1947. David, the man after God's own heart, made not a few errors of judgment in his time through failing "to seek the Lord" and leaning to his own understanding. Watchman Nee, it appears, was in this venture no wiser than David.

When the Sino-Japanese war ended in 1945, Dr. Yu, one of the Hardoon Road leaders and an eye surgeon, tried to get the meetings going again. But it was not until Witness Lee came from Chefoo to Shanghai to reorganize and reconstitute the assembly that assembly life really revived. Watchman Nee was still in disgrace. However, the wartime pattern of fifteen separate centres for "breaking of bread" was continued.

In 1947 Watchman Nee was received back into fellowship, though already his active brain had been thinking about future methods of working and articles on the subject of the "Church" and the "ministry" were pouring from his pen. In May 1948 Witness Lee staged a huge "fellowship meeting" in Shanghai to cement the reconciliation that had taken place. Indeed, in 1948 Watchman Nee was at the height of his influence and popular regard. All over China he had his followers and admirers, while in Shanghai a new meeting place was being built in Nanyang Road to hold 3,000 people. The Hardoon Road premises had become far too small to accommodate the large congregations. On completion, the new hall was often filled for the ministry of the Word, while the congregation continued the wartime practice of meeting separately for the "breaking of bread" in numerous localities and private homes around the city. Among Mr. Nee's colleagues were

men of considerable ability and spirituality. But Mr.
Nee himself stood out above them all, a man of great
intellect, great personal charm and charisma. Almost
inevitably a cult of hero-worship developed. Stephen
Chan in his memoirs[1] recalls, "Before 1948 I was very
enthusiastic about the assemblies. . . . I loved to read
my uncle's books and bought everything published
by the Gospel Book Room. But when I returned
home to Foochow in 1948 I was greatly disappointed
and had the feeling that there were those in the
assembly who certainly worshipped God but also
worshipped their idol Brother Nee. One constantly
heard the phrase 'Brother Nee says this . . . or that
. . .'. They did not say 'God's Word says this . . . or
that . . .'. It was as if Brother Nee's words had been
given more authority than Holy Scripture. . . . To
exalt one of like passions as oneself to the place of
God is a sin. . . . Because he accepted so much adula-
tion God allowed him to suffer defeat." It became
possible almost always to detect Little Flock
Christians by their mannerisms: at one period the
typical clicking sound they made when praying was
an unconscious imitation of the sound made by Mr.
Nee's imperfectly fitting dentures! What is sad is the
fact that again there was no one of sufficient stature
to challenge Nee's views and help him sort out his
prejudices from his insight. "Handing over" was an
essential part of his preaching emphasis in 1948.

With some of the wealth which had poured into
the Little Flock treasury as hundreds of Christians
"handed over" their possessions to the church, Mr.
Nee purchased a large residence in Foochow with
extensive grounds and gardens and some holiday
bungalows in the hills at Kuliang, outside Foochow.

[1] *My Uncle, Nee To-sheng* by Stephen Chan.

He made necessary alterations to the buildings to provide a hostel for the accommodation of workers who came to Foochow for training. Again, in the original version of *Concerning Our Missions* we find Mr. Nee opposed to workers (or "apostles") exercising authority in the local church. He insisted that this authority should be exercised by the local elders alone. In the local church "workers" were to be no other than ordinary members. Their function was to engage in a ministry serving all the churches. If they were by any chance not received by a local church they were to accept this in humility and, if so led, engage in their ministry of evangelism there, but on no account to form a rival meeting or church. This, Mr. Nee insisted, was forbidden by Scripture.

But it appears that 1948 marked a turning point in Mr. Nee's church practices and the beginning of an hierarchical system of central control which differed little from the organization of denominational churches. There are those who believe that here we are witnessing the growing influence of Witness Lee, who later was to exercise such autocratic control over the churches in Taiwan. The original Foochow assembly was still under the leadership of Mr. Chang Ch'i-chen, one of the original founders with Mr. Nee of that assembly back in 1923. But by 1928, owing to disagreements, a second meeting place had been started with its own responsible elders and its own autonomous government. The one "church" in Foochow met in two places, to the distress and embarrassment of Mr. Nee and the assemblies in Shanghai and elsewhere. They continued to hope and pray that this schism might be healed.

Later in 1947 Watchman Nee and Witness Lee visited assemblies in Fukien and Kuangtung for the purpose of renewed fellowship. Then in February 1948 a special conference met in Foochow when Mr. Nee, Mr. Lee and twenty-seven fellow-workers gathered. Together they perceived a new principle of witness. In 1937 they had adopted the "Antioch Principle", the going forth of apostles, and now it was to be the "Jerusalem Principle", the going forth of scattered saints, according to which an entire group of believers would voluntarily migrate or be forcibly moved by persecution from one well-established church centre to found a new church witness in an unevangelized area. This was what had already taken place in Chefoo in 1933 with remarkable success under Witness Lee's leadership. With this vision clear, all the workers "handed themselves over" to fulfil it and decided to make Foochow their Jerusalem, the administrative centre of "the work". Their slogan was to be "China for Christ in five years!" This was on March 3rd.

Obviously it would be desirable to have a united church at the base. The newer assembly expressed its willingness to "hand itself over" to the team of workers but the original assembly proved quite unwilling to yield its autonomy in spite of several deputations of senior workers sent to persuade them to do so. The twenty-seven workers were firmly rebuffed and the schism in Foochow became permanent. Watchman Nee and Witness Lee issued a full statement about the schism in a special leaflet for the information of all Little Flock assemblies.

What is clear is that Mr. Nee and the Little Flock leadership had gone back on their original principles as set out in the first edition of *Concerning Our Missions*. They had sought to deprive the original local assembly in Foochow of its autonomy and to

establish "worker" control in place of "elder control"
in a local church, on the ground that the "church" is
local while the "work" is regional. Thus the post-
1948 era saw a change of direction or rather an
important stage in the evolution in Little Flock
thinking and policies which necessitated a revised
edition of *Concerning Our Missions*. (In 1961 the Little
Flock headquarters in Taiwan published yet another
revised edition which was said to represent "new
light" seen since 1948. The purpose of this latest
edition seems to have been to reconcile the pre-1948
and the post-1948 contradictions.)

A start was made with putting into operation the
"Jerusalem Principle", and some groups of families
did pull up their roots in Shanghai and elsewhere to
migrate to unevangelized areas. But already the
hour was too late. On October 1st, 1949, Chairman
Mao Tse-tung, following successive military victories,
including the capture of Peking, Nanking and
Shanghai, declared the establishment of the People's
Republic of China. The days of freedom of action
for the Christian churches were over.

In April 1950 the Communist *Liberation Daily*
reported on a sermon Watchman Nee had preached
at a Little Flock conference in Shanghai on the text
"Render unto God the things that are God's".
Clearly, both Watchman Nee and the assembly
were heading for trouble.

11 *Imprisonment*

In late 1950 the China Inland Mission's leadership decided to withdraw its missionaries from China. They were the last missionary society to do so. The advice of their Chinese colleagues and friends was almost unanimous. The continued presence of missionaries could only be an embarrassment and a hindrance to the Chinese Church which was being accused of being a tool of western imperialism. The exodus began in early 1951.

But before the C.I.M. leaders left, Mr. Watchman Nee and his colleagues in the Little Flock accepted an invitation to the C.I.M. Headquarters in Sinza Road for a morning of fellowship and prayer. By this time the work of Mr. Nee had been fully recognized as a significant contribution to the total work of God in China, though its divisions and some of its doctrinal emphases still caused sorrow to Mr. Nee's friends and well-wishers. But the bitterness of earlier years, when several C.I.M. missionaries and some in other missions had been persuaded to leave the Mission's ranks, and when many churches founded by the C.I.M. had been taken over by the Little Flock movement, was now a thing of the past. The foreign missionary organizations in China were disbanding and the Chinese Church was facing a grim future.

"How long will this suffering continue?" queried one of the guests.

"It has scarcely begun," was the reply. "Much worse is bound to follow!"

During the course of the conversation one of the hosts asked Mr. Nee how he thought missionaries could best serve the Chinese Church in the future.

"First of all," was the immediate answer, "provide us with Bible commentaries. You have so many and we have so few. Translate Bishop Lightfoot's commentaries, for example, and other similar works. And then, when you can come back again, come not as evangelists but as teaching elders in our local churches. You will receive a very warm welcome."

And after these memorable requests the Christian brethren from East and West prayed together and bade one another goodbye. Now the hour had come for this influential leader whom the Communists were determined to silence.

Soon the "accusation campaign", launched in April 1951 at the Peking Conference, where the Three-Self Reform Movement was inaugurated, was in full swing—just at the time when missionaries were pouring out of China. On April 27th sixteen thousand arrests were made in Shanghai alone and among them were some Christians. Then on June 10th a mass accusation meeting at the Shanghai Canidrome Stadium at which every Christian organization in the city was represented, purported to expose the crimes of the "American imperialists" in using the Christian Church for its aggression in China. The meeting received nation-wide publicity in the daily press. In 1952 the "Five Anti-" campaign was launched, the five enemies being bribery, smuggling, stealing national resources, skimping on work and material and stealing national economic reports. Already Little Flock members had been found to accuse their leader and the organization. So the next step was the arrest of Mr. Watchman Nee who was accused of all five crimes and in addition of gross immorality. The court sentenced him to twenty years' imprisonment. Three years later, on January 21st, 1956, the four elders of the Little Flock assembly in Shanghai who had carried the pastoral responsibilities after Mr. Nee's imprisonment, together with twenty-eight other Christian leaders in the Shanghai area, were also arrested. On January 30th, two thousand five hundred Little Flock members were summoned to a mass denunciation meeting. The chairman declared that the Little Flock itself was not a counter-revolutionary movement but that counter-revolutionaries were hiding in it, and these the government were determined to root out. Two days later eight hundred Shanghai Christians attended a meeting to assure the government of their united support for the arrest and punishment of Watchman Nee. The admittedly short-lived practice by the Little Flock of "handing over" all private possessions came under severe criticism. Once again the daily press gave the meeting wide publicity and represented Watchman Nee to the world as an utterly corrupt individual. Soon after this the Little Flock, now considered purged of its alleged rebellion, joined the Three-Self Patriotic Movement.

In China itself the Little Flock Movement like every other branch of the Chinese Church is at present underground, but in Hong Kong, in Taiwan, in Singapore, in the Philippines and (who knows?) in China too, the testimony which Watchman Nee originated is being maintained, a testimony to holy living and the corporate witness of the local church.

In prison Mr. Nee's unique abilities were

harnessed to translation work for the government.
Rumours kept cropping up about his death and even
of his mutilation, but all were untrue. Little Flock
members in Shanghai knew the facts and Mrs. Nee
was allowed to visit her husband from time to time.
In the autumn of 1971 Mrs. Nee, already suffering
from a weak heart, had a serious fall. She died a few
days later, but not before her sister could reach her
from Peking. After the funeral Mr. Nee's sister-in-law
visited him in his labour camp and found that he had
already been informed of his wife's death. In his grief
he was calm and triumphant. Some time in April
1972 Mr. Nee was released from the labour camp
near Shanghai and transferred to an open centre in
the province of Anhwei. He had long suffered from
a heart complaint and life was difficult for him in the
new environment, but on May 22nd, 1972, he wrote
to his sister-in-law in Peking reporting his poor
health, yet declaring that "the inward joy surpasses
everything" and expressing the hope that she too
shared this joy. Ten days later, on June 1st, Nee
Duo-sheng, affectionately known all over the world
as Watchman Nee, went to be "with Christ which is
far better". His long drawn out suffering in mind and
body were over. Despite pressures of every kind he
never denied his Lord or renounced his faith. To the
end he was true to his God.

Let the final assessment of Watchman Nee's life
be that of a Chinese, the nephew who wrote his
memoirs: "The great thing about so many spiritual
people is not that they never knew defeat or weakness.
The Bible does not cover up the records of the failures
of many spiritual people who were used by God—
people like Abraham, Moses or Miriam. Their
failures are all recorded because God does not fail to

confront us with the whole truth about people. Thus we, seeing the greatness of the achievements and the praiseworthiness of a person, will recognize how in the wonderful wisdom of God He can use a worthless vessel to fulfil His will. My uncle had his manifold faults and failings, but these do not nullify the fact that he was greatly used of God. He was one of many humble people and by no means perfect, yet he was certainly one whom God used. He was a vessel unto honour."[1]

[1] *ibid.*

PART 3

WANG MING-DAO

Man of Iron

1 *Boxer Year*

1900 was a memorable year for the Wang family. In the Chinese Calendar it was the Year of the Rat. The year began calmly enough, though the severe drought affecting North China and now in its third year was constantly in the news. Two successive crop failures, locust swarms and Yellow River floods had caused severe famine. Dr. Wang De-hao was employed at the Methodist Hospital just inside the Hatamen Gate in the south of the Tartar City of Peking. His wife, Li Wen-yi who had studied in a London Missionary Society school, had already given birth to four children, of whom only a daughter was still living, and was again pregnant.

Peking at the end of the nineteenth century was even more a place of beauty, grandeur and ceremonial than it is today. The city had originally been built by the Mongol conquerors of China in the thirteenth century. The fifteen miles of stone wall surrounding the Tartar City were high and in perfect condition. Inside that city was the Imperial City with its six miles of red walls within which the government offices were located, while at the heart of the Imperial City stood the fabulous Imperial Palace protected by a wide moat and substantial walls pierced by only one gate. This was the domain of Tzu-hsi, the Empress Dowager, who had ruled the land as Regent for virtually thirty-nine years, first during the minority of her young son and again after having deposed him

from the Dragon Throne. Outside the South Wall of
the Tartar City lay the Chinese city, a fascinating
place with street names indicating the variety of
Chinese handicrafts—Jade Street, Lantern Street,
Street of the Silversmiths, Flower and Bead Street,
Embroidery Street, Street of the Brass and Copper-
smiths, Silk Street. There, too, was one of Peking's
greatest glories, the azure roofed three-tiered Temple
of Heaven and the gleaming white marble Altar of
Heaven, on which the emperors, called "Sons of
Heaven", annually offered sacrifices on behalf of
their people to Heaven itself, with all the elaborate
ceremonial of ancient tradition. Peking abounded in
historic temples, beautiful homes, quiet *"hutungs"*,
princely palaces and lovely parks. All the year round
it provided an ever-changing panorama of colourful
festivals. In 1900 the Imperial Palace was still a
"forbidden city"—forbidden to all except the
imperial family and entourage.

But the ancient capital was restless. In 1895 China
had been disastrously defeated in a war with Japan.
Now for the past ten years the insolent aggression
of the western nations had become increasingly
intolerable. The "foreign devils" had been "carving
up the melon" or delineating for themselves spheres
of influence in China. Russia, Japan, Germany,
France and Great Britain were all equally guilty.
Already the Dowager Empress had suppressed the
Reform Movement. What had China to learn from
western barbarians with their high-handed, aggressive actions against the sacred soil of China? And
now there was this terrible drought in Shansi,
Shensi and parts of Chihli. The Empress's Taoist
advisers recommended the shedding of human blood
to appease the gods of the soil and so end the famine,

while her political advisers were in favour of ridding China of all "foreign devils", who had brought nothing but trouble to China. And this included the missionaries. In 1900 there were five hundred foreign residents in Peking, half of these being missionaries.

And so the pale green of the willows by the palace moat gave way to the peach and cherry blossoms and the spring flowers were succeeded by the peonies of early summer. When the British celebrated the anniversary of Queen Victoria's accession on May 24th there was no premonition of the coming storm in spite of the murder of two Catholic and three Protestant missionaries in Shantung in April. Suddenly, rumours began to cause increasing alarm, especially among the Christians. The secret society, the Yi He Tuan (Society of the Righteous Fist), commonly called "Boxers", was training its detachments in the use of death-dealing swords. Its members believed themselves to be immune against rifle bullets. They were awaiting the Imperial Decree empowering them to move against the hated foreign population. Murderous attacks on Catholics and Protestants took place in the Peking region. Europeans hastened to Peking to take refuge in the Legation quarter. On May 28th, the Diplomatic Corps asked Tientsin for guards. Tension grew as the reinforcement arrived and as huge mobs surrounded the Legations. Boxer atrocities were being committed on innocent Peking citizens. On June 19th U.S. Marines rescued seventy-six American missionaries and converts from the Methodist compound. Dr. Wang and his family were among them. The Chinese Christians were accommodated in the grounds and residence of Prince Su, now a part of the Legation Quarter. On June 20th the siege of the

Legations began. The defence force numbered three
hundred and eighty-nine men and twenty officers.
Seeing the violence of the Boxer soldiers and fearing
humiliation at their hands Dr. Wang, utterly
distraught with fear and strain, killed himself at the
end of June. His shocked and sorrowing wife was
within a month of her time and on July 25th her
fifth child, a son, was born. No midwife being
available to deliver the baby, the grandmother
performed the task.

For all who endured the siege, foreigners and
Chinese alike, it was a harrowing experience.
Eventually, after fifty-five days, the Legations were
relieved on August 14th by an Allied Expeditionary
Force which fought its way through to Peking from
the treaty port city of Tientsin. Tsu-hsi and her court
fled to the old national capital of Sian, leaving
Peking at the mercy of the foreign troops who for the
second time in forty years indulged in an orgy of loot
and destruction, particularly in the lovely Summer
Palace of the emperors near the foot of the Western
Hills. Chinese and foreigners gradually drifted back
to their homes to assess their losses. But Mrs. Wang
and her two children no longer had any home to
which to return. With the silver with which she was
compensated, Mrs. Wang bought a house in Gan-yu
Hutung (Precious Rain Street) where she earned a
little money by renting out a few rooms to lodgers.
She herself was an undomesticated woman who
disliked cooking. Consequently her family was poorly
fed and the children began to suffer from malnutrition. Moreover, being a quick tempered woman,
her relations with her neighbours were far from
happy and noisy altercations were frequent. The
people living in the same courtyard were little more

than riff-raff, people with low morals who soon corrupted the new addition to the Wang family.

2 *Childhood*

"Wang Number One" had been given the name of Tie, or Iron, because he was a lusty baby. So his pet name became "Iron Child" or "Iron Son", though his weakness through malnutrition belied the name and his childhood was marred by frequent sickness. At an early age "Tie-zi" was determined to help his mother eke out a living and used to go with her every morning before school, basket over his arm, to collect coal and cinders from the refuse dumps of nearby wealthy homes.

Thanks to the family's Christian associations a Bible and a hymnbook were among the few family possessions. Curiosity led young Tie-zi to examine them as soon as he was able to read. The Bible raised questions in the boy's mind such as, "What do men live for?"; "After death what?" When he talked to his uncle, who was a Buddhist, about these problems, the only advice offered was that he should enter a monastery so as to avoid death.

When the boy was nine his mother sent him to the L.M.S. Cui Wen Primary School with the new "school" name of Yung-sheng, or Eternal Abundance. For the first time he was able to get away from the evil environment of his home which was already making its mark on his own language and conduct. But at school he soon found other boys whose behaviour was as bad as his own. He lacked only the money and the courage to share their indulgences. Though the school authorities were strict as to discipline, religion was formal and the boys were not taught how to live. However, Yung-sheng proved to be above average intelligence and this, combined with hard work, kept him at the top of his class and first in examinations. It was a great relief to his mother when he was awarded a scholarship which covered the cost of his board and lodgings.

Writing at a later date of his own character Mr. Wang said, "In me there are two instincts—one conservative and the other radical. If I considered a thing to be unalterable then not a shade of it could I allow to be altered. But if I considered a thing to be alterable then it must be altered thoroughly. Because of the presence of these two instincts many people were annoyed with me from my youth onwards and I too had to suffer for them."

The Nationalist Revolution profoundly affected Peking. In 1912 the boy emperor Pu-yi abdicated and so ended the Manchu Dynasty, the last of many dynasties stretching back into antiquity. The revolutionary government declared Nanking to be the new capital of China and so Peking lost much of its importance and glamour as the heart of a great imperial power. Schoolboys like Wang Yung-sheng were soon accustomed to raising the new Nationalist flag daily and singing the new National Anthem "*San Min Zhu-i*", "The Three Principles of the People". If young Wang had had his way things would have been altered more radically than they actually were!

3 Conversion

Despite the want of true spiritual help at the church school where Yung-sheng was studying, one senior boy in particular began to exercise a strong influence over the younger. He was a strong and well-taught Christian who was able to teach his young friend and to lead him into a clear experience of faith in Christ. He also taught him to pray, to study the Bible and to keep a diary in which he recorded his spiritual progress. This was in the springtime of his fourteenth year—in 1914. Of his conversion Yung-sheng recorded in his diary: "From that day I had a belief, a purpose in life, a reforming passion and I ceased to live out my days aimlessly. Nevertheless a war continued in my heart between the two principles of good and evil and this was a painful experience." His school-mate gave his young friend a book by H. L. Zia of the Y.M.C.A. entitled *A Help to Personal Development* which laid strong emphasis on practical Christian living. This book strongly influenced the whole trend of Mr. Wang's life and teaching. "Every time I erred in speech or conduct I would be grieved and reproached in heart, shedding tears over my sins which I confessed before God."

During Yung-sheng's second year of high school his older friend, who had been such a tower of strength to him, graduated, leaving him to bear his faithful witness alone. He soon met with persecution from a few wealthy, loose-living companions who nicknamed him "the doctor of theology" and were always looking for opportunities to call him a Pharisee when they detected some inconsistency in his speech or conduct. As a result of these experiences he found himself walking a narrow pathway.

At fifteen Yung-sheng had made up his mind what to do. "I determined to become a politician because I had observed from history and the daily press that politicians were esteemed above all other people." The aspiring politician had read the life of Abraham Lincoln which encouraged him with the knowledge that even a person from a humble background like his own could achieve greatness. Lincoln became his hero and his picture hung on Yung-sheng's bedroom wall. His ambition led him to study hard, live irreproachably and serve the Lord fervently.

But as the boy grew in Christian experience a rival ambition entered his life—to be a preacher. Yung-sheng had qualities that would serve him well in either calling; he had been born in Peking, the cultural heart of China, he was a gifted writer and he had a good speaking voice. For four years the conflict went on between those two ambitions. His controversy with God seemed unending. At eighteen he was ready to enter university. That was the year when the first world war came to an end and China was humiliated by the terms of the Peace Treaty and the aggressive designs of Japan. Student agitation flared up everywhere, especially in Peking, while anti-Japanese boycotts and strikes seriously disrupted the economic life of the country. Wang's own health was poor but his mother's was worse, so he felt an obligation to discontinue his education in order to help his mother at home.

Clearly a university course was essential if Wang

was to attain either of his ambitions. But Yenching University did not accept him and as he was in the process of applying to Cheloo University in Shantung he was offered a post at a Presbyterian Primary School in Baoding at a salary of twelve dollars a month. The uncertainty about his future had been a trying experience. Indeed it had induced a severe illness lasting a month. But now his course seemed well set and the period of darkness ended. His political ambition had been set aside. On September 11th, 1918, he left home for his new sphere of work, some eighty miles south on the Peking–Hankow mainline.

Wang was by now an established Christian and still an enthusiastic disciple of H. L. Zia whose ideals he tried to apply in his work as a teacher. He also set them before his pupils for whom he arranged prayer meetings, Bible study groups and a voluntary social service group. But Wang's own understanding of Scripture was still somewhat confused. In the staff room he found the company uncongenial and far from Christian, though he soon earned the respect of the boys and even won popularity with them.

In 1920 the long conflict of ambition was resolved. Wang had surrendered his will to God and given up all thoughts of a political career. He was seriously considering entering a theological college. To mark this event he adopted a new name—Mingdao, or "Witness to the Truth". The news of the conversion of his sister gave Wang an added joy. But he was receiving little spiritual encouragement in the Baoding church and it was left to a friend to speak to him faithfully about the need for true repentance and confession of sin to God. On November 21st he searched his heart, wrote out a list of his sins to

confess to God and for the first time received full
assurance of forgiveness.

Wang had already been baptized after the
Congregational fashion at the Peking school. But in
1921 he became exercised about being baptized as a
believer. After discussing the subject at length with
his friends, he finally decided to be baptized by
immersion. When he notified the Presbyterian school
authorities of his intention, however, he was
threatened with dismissal if he went through with
them. Re-baptism may be a dubious practice, but
Wang's mind was made up. Five of the Christian
boys in the school also made the decision to leave
over this issue, among them Shih Tian-min, his
lifelong friend and colleague. The fateful day was
January 5th in the depth of a north China winter.
The whole land was in the grip of intense frost and
rivers were frozen over. Not even this could deter the
young zealots who broke the ice of a stream in order
to be baptized. They firmly believed they were
acting in obedience to God's command. (Years later,
Wang was invited back by the same missionary
authorities to preach in Baoding.)

Soon after these events, the six young Christians
came under the influence of an older Chinese who
urged them to "pray for the Holy Spirit". In their
zeal for God's best they did so and all six "spoke
with tongues". Wang, however, soon decided that
his experience had not been of God and he never
sought a repetition. But it was a Pentecostal missionary from Sweden, Eric Pilquist, who in February
1923 led Wang into a clearer understanding of the
truth of salvation through faith alone. "Faith alone",
however, was never more than half the truth for
Wang, who set himself to hate evil and to demand

from every professing Christian the fruits of justification in holiness of living.

Wang was now out of a job, and he returned home to find his mother and sister thoroughly disapproving of the step he had taken in giving up a good post. Even his best friends showed little sympathy. He seemed to have made enemies for himself on all sides. The words of 1 Corinthians 10.13 became his strength and comfort: "There hath no temptation taken you but such as is common to man: but God is faithful, who will not suffer you to be tempted above that ye are able; but will with the temptation also make a way to escape, that ye may be able to bear it." Having nothing in particular to do, he undertook the housework at home and began a serious study of the Bible.

4 A Growing Ministry

1921 was the year in which the Chinese Communist Party was founded. The Christian Church soon came under attack throughout the nation, but the reactions of the mainline churches to criticism and opposition did not commend themselves to Wang, who began to gain a reputation for fearlessness and outspokenness in his own criticisms. This reputation was to remain with him all his life. For a time he was so disturbed that some people even suggested he was mentally ill. Years later he attributed his condition to the conflict between a desire to follow the Lord wholly and an immature, prejudiced attitude. What he needed was quiet, to get to grips with himself and to wait on God.

Just at the right time, an older cousin who was a military doctor invited Wang to stay at his country home outside Peking in a village near the Summer Palace in the Western Hills. There, for sixty-two days, he found peace amid the mountains and the streams and there he spent long periods in prayer and the study of the Bible. This was Wang's "Arabia", his own personal training school. Returning to Peking he met one of his friends, Mr. Chen Zi-hao, who had once been most critical. Mr. Chen now recognized that Wang was not out of his mind, but rather that the grace of God was resting upon him.

On the 2nd of July Wang preached his first public sermon in Chen's church at Zang Xien. The subject of this maiden sermon set the pattern for all Wang's future preaching. "Repent for the Kingdom of Heaven is at hand". A further month's preaching in Yen Xien and Xiang-shou set the seal on Wang's call to the ministry of God's Word, though the missionaries objected to a suggestion that he might extend his preaching for a further three months. Wang now knew in his own heart that God had both chosen him and given him the gifts and the ability to be His servant. He was twenty-two years of age.

While waiting for God to open the doors for service, there were lessons to be learned in the school of humility. He still had no regular employment and no permanent means of livelihood, and he felt rebellious against God for not immediately providing opportunities for service. Instead, God shut up this firebrand to menial tasks in order to prepare the instrument that was to rebuke sin both in the Church and in the world. Wang found himself confined within his own home where he learned to perform the humdrum daily chores with extreme conscientiousness and thoroughness. Never were floors kept cleaner, or furniture better polished. The day's work done, he spent hours poring over his Bible and seeking to understand its teaching more perfectly. He was learning to be nothing—neither politician nor preacher—if God so willed. Those were his hidden years.

In August 1923 Wang emerged from his eighteen months' silent discipline to lead an eight-day conference in Zan Huang at the invitation of the China Inland Mission. Thereafter invitations followed thick and fast.

The Christian Church in China in the early twenties was facing a severe test of strength but showed many signs of weakness. The comparatively rapid growth of the first decade of the century after the Boxer uprising had proved in many instances too superficial. Some of the converts of those years were now senior members and even pastors in churches, though often lacking any depth of Christian experience. Consequently both among the preachers and the rank and file of Christians there was the plague of nominal Christianity accompanied by low standards of conduct. For this, rightly or wrongly, Wang blamed the missionaries for not understanding the Chinese. It was they, he said, who had been taken in by "rice Christians" and self-seekers. It was they who had accepted unbelievers into the churches. It was they who had selected the brighter students in the schools for theological training, regardless of their spiritual qualifications, and even sent them to America for advanced training, often in liberal colleges. In this way false shepherds who demanded

salaries the churches could not afford to pay had
infiltrated the churches. Wang's own unsatisfactory
experience in denominational schools and at the
hands of foreign missionaries had induced him to
make sweeping statements of this kind. Inevitably
his attitude ensured that his own life work was to be
outside that of the foreign denominations. His was to
be an independent (though not separatist) and
individual ministry. His standpoint would always be
an independent one in relation to the over-all church
situation in China.

On the 4th of March, 1924, Wang was invited to
join a team of thirty Chinese and missionaries in a
six-day mission in an army camp at Nan-yuan, the
first such close association in service Wang had had
with Western missionaries and their Chinese colleagues. He was not impressed. On the contrary he
wrote bluntly and very sweepingly, "Most missionaries are really unworthy to be called the servants of
Christ. This experience made me more than ever
aware of the corruption, the vanity, the poverty and
the pity of the churches in China and I am even
more moved to be zealous in the Lord's service."

Later that same year, in August, Wang Ming-dao
was invited to attend a leaders' conference of
American and British Congregationalists at Te Xien.
At one session the speaker spoke disparagingly of the
Scriptures in a way which tended to undermine the
faith of believers. Wang Ming-dao was deeply
disturbed and after earnest prayer he boldly and
publicly argued against the former speaker's errors,
only to bring down on his head the wrath of his
opponents. This was Wang's first major clash with
those disruptive elements in the Church which were
to become the constant targets of his attack through-

out his whole life. At the time he was still but a youth of twenty-four. The experience drove him to a more intense study of the Scriptures in his own home. "I accept," he said, "all that is written in the Scriptures and what I cannot find written there I shall leave aside. I believe all the Truth that is written in the Scriptures and am unwilling to accept the reasonings that are not found in Scripture."

5 *Marriage and a New Church*

That autumn Wang Ming-dao decided to start holding Bible classes in his own home at Precious Rain Street. The first meeting was in mid-October 1924. Growing numbers were attracted to hear the eloquent young preacher and it was soon necessary to transfer the services to the home of an influential lady who was his enthusiastic admirer. In spite of this potential competitor, several ministers of Peking churches were glad to invite Wang Ming-dao to fill their pulpits, for he was already a man with a message that Christians needed and wanted to hear. Wang now saw himself as a present-day Jeremiah with a ministry to rebuke the sins of the Church regardless of the consequences or of his own popularity. He was aware that while some would accept him others would oppose. And he was not mistaken. During the twenty years beginning in 1925 Wang Ming-dao covered China in his journeys, visiting twenty-four of the twenty-eight provinces, commencing with Fukien, Chekiang and Kiangsi. In 1926 and

1927 he was away from home for over six months in each year. Over thirty missions and church groups were glad to welcome this man with a message. In spite of his fears to the contrary he was invited back time and again, though he had plenty of critics.

About this time, too, Wang Ming-dao made the first beginnings in a literary output which was to assume considerable dimensions. His first published booklets had these titles, *A Most Important Matter, A Cry amid the Evil World, Christians and Idols, Who is Jesus?* and *The Cross of Christ.* The titles themselves indicate the polemic character of his early works. Then in the spring of 1927, after a journey to Nanking to meet other like-minded friends, the periodical which was to continue publication for more than twenty-five years was launched, *Spiritual Food Quarterly.* Because he believed that the ministry of this magazine was so important, he set aside definite periods to be in Peking to write and to publish. With only small resources in money and manpower he kept the magazine going right up to the very end. Over the years its pages reproduced his own sermons and Scripture expositions. These have since been perpetuated in a library of about thirty books printed in Hong Kong. *Spiritual Food Quarterly* eventually achieved a nation-wide circulation and had an enormous influence—an influence which in the end forced the Communists to silence its voice.

The visit to Nanking which led to the launching of *Spiritual Food Quarterly* was not all pleasure. His preaching there offended some, but opposition was a healthy check to the pride which remained near the surface and a popularity which could only have done him harm.

Before returning to the north he paid a visit to the

lovely and historic city of Hangchow where he was a guest in the house of Pastor Liu. This proved to be a really momentous occasion for in Pastor Liu's daughter Wang Ming-dao met his future wife, a charming practical person, ideally suited for the burdens and sacrifices of an evangelist's wife. The couple were married in 1928. Their only child, a son, Tian-du was born two years later.

Family ties did not keep Wang Ming-dao at home. In 1931 he paid his first visits to Hong Kong and Macao, and in the following year he took five long journeys to several provinces. Then, in 1932, he was away from home for eight long months comprising six preaching tours, and was a leading speaker at the Kuling and Bei-dai-he Summer Conferences. He also found time for a prolonged visit to Manchuria and, at the urgent request of Pastor David Yang Shao-t'ang of Shansi, he conducted meetings there time and time again. Everywhere his preaching was used to uncover sin and to bring nominal Christians to deep repentance and a living faith in Christ. Revival in the churches was a fairly general feature in the early thirties. But revival was accompanied by many disturbing extremes and satanic counterfeits which led Wang Ming-dao to publish his discussion of *Spiritual Gifts* and an exposition of *The New Birth*, both in 1933.

Meanwhile in Peking the work was growing apace. His own home became inadequate to accommodate all those who wanted to attend the services, so two other homes were opened for worship and Bible study, one of them accommodating one hundred and fifty and the other three hundred people. Mr. Wang was continually being urged to consider building a permanent place of worship and in 1934 a fund was finally started for this purpose. In 1936 there was enough money to purchase a property at No. 42 in the street known as Shih Jia Hutung. The existing building was demolished and a spacious church to hold seven hundred built in its place. For the purpose of buying land and registering the building with the government it was necessary for the property to have a name. Mr. Wang prayed much about this and decided on "The Christian Tabernacle". Only those who could give evidence of repentance, faith and regeneration, shown by a radical change in their lives and conduct, were accepted for baptism. Some applicants had to wait for as long as three years before meeting the requirements. As the Chinese proverb goes, "Better a few good things than many bad ones". Wang Ming-dao did not choose to assume the title "pastor". He was never known by any other title than "Xien-sheng" or "Mr". He reckoned himself as among the deacons, who, with the stewards, were the church's controlling body. These men were selected first of all on the basis of the genuineness of their faith and exemplary conduct, then of their talents, knowledge and scholarship. Financial status was never considered. To his colleagues Mr. Wang was familiarly known as "Ming-dao" and to the younger generation as "Brother Ming-dao". Teenagers delighted to call him "Uncle". The fellowship at Shih Jia Hutung was just like a large family. No worker earned a salary. Offering boxes were available to receive gifts earmarked for individuals or for general purposes. The form of worship was extremely simple and without any kind of liturgy. Mr. Wang never countenanced even a choir, lest talented singers who were not God-fearing people should find in this the opportunity to exalt themselves and their talents and so debase true worship.

During the building operations Mr. Wang held a Spring conference in 1936, before setting off on another four and a half months of journeys, everywhere preaching with power and conviction. The new building was finally completed in July 1937, just as the clash between Chinese and Japanese troops at the Marco Polo Bridge outside Peking detonated the eight-year-long Sino-Japanese War. The city was soon occupied and Mr. Wang cancelled his autumn engagements.

The new church building was dedicated to the service of God on August 1st. It was simple in design and furnishing and devoid of all Christian art or symbols—not even a cross inside or out! On the white marble foundation stone were inscribed these words,

> He died for our sins.
> He rose from the dead.
> He ascended to heaven.
> He will come again to receive us.
> 1937, Summer

The interior walls were white, while the platform, lectern and chairs were grey. The baptistry was in the centre in front of the pulpit.

Once the new congregation in its own place of worship was fully operative Mr. Wang resumed his preaching tours throughout North China, in spite of the prevailing war conditions. In his absence he used to leave Mr. Shih Tian-min, his old school friend, in charge as his deputy. Few other preachers ever occupied the pulpit and never once a foreigner, as far as is known.

Mr. Wang was eloquent in the beautiful, lilting Peking dialect. He was never dull to listen to. He was a true evangelist in his clear presentation of salvation through faith alone, repentance and the new birth of the Spirit. Thousands must have been brought to true faith in Christ through the evangelistic preaching. But Mr. Wang was equally outstanding for being a preacher of righteousness to Christians. He held no dogmatic views about "sanctification", but never wearied of insisting on holy living for every believer. He was ruthless in denouncing the sins and inconsistencies of Christians. His standards were very high and even flew in the face of Chinese traditional etiquette which he pronounced to be hypocritical and dishonest in many respects. For example, if a host had provided a specially good meal he found it out of keeping with Christian morality to apologize to his guests for having provided "no meat and vegetables", even though this was the customary polite thing to say. In insisting on absolute honesty he probed every department of life, but what is more, the man himself was a man of utter integrity, a man without guile. Unlike some of his contemporaries his public and private life were completely free of any breath of scandal. Never did a whiff of suspicion touch his social relationships and even his bitterest enemies could find "no fault in him" except in the sphere of his uncompromising stand when it came to the issues of truth or error. Here he waged a lifelong crusade against the spread of liberal theology in China and never minced his words in referring to those Chinese leaders who were prominent among the liberals in the Chinese Church, denouncing them in no uncertain terms. Here was a stern, severe John the Baptist when it came to what he believed to be error of any kind and he never spared those responsible in his public utterances and in his circulated writings.

Mr. Wang held many individual missionaries, proud to be among his friends, in respect. But he was strong in his criticism of the missionary movement as a whole for reasons already given, especially the sending abroad for further theological education of selected students. Mr. Wang himself spoke and read English well, but he refused every invitation to go abroad to be lionized by a flattering Christian public. He had seen too many good men spoilt by this treatment. He neither sought nor wanted patronage or financial backing from any foreign sources. He was proudly and independently Chinese.

6 *First Confrontation*

The war against Japan was always one-sided. Japan had a far superior air, sea and land force with all the most modern weapons. China was still, in many respects, in the sword and hand-to-hand combat stage. Her gallant armies were defeated and driven back inexorably though not without some notable victories which upset the Japanese programme. Province after province was occupied and remained occupied for six or seven years and experienced the bitterness of enemy occupation. The capture and rape of Nanking horrified the civilized world as the victorious Japanese troops behaved in brutal and bestial fashion. Universities hastily packed their libraries and scientific equipment in crates and transported them by river or overland to the mountainous provinces of the west, there to ride out the war in freedom and to continue higher education even under the most primitive conditions in temples or temporary buildings in often remote towns and villages. As the regular combat troops of the Nationalist armies withdrew their lines steadily westward, guerilla troops of the Communist armies remained behind in Japanese occupied territory to harass enemy communication, so making this occupation as difficult and as costly as possible.

Then in 1941 the Japanese went to war with the Western powers already at war with Germany. Western nationals in Japanese occupied territory immediately found themselves in danger and were eventually interned. The Japanese also imposed controls on all "Western" institutions. In fact, all churches sponsored by Great Britain or the U.S.A. were ordered to close and the Japanese set up a puppet organization known as "The Society for the Support of the Christian Churches of Peking", to arrange for their co-operative and independent function. Mr. Wang Ming-dao was invited to attend the inaugural meeting, but he refused the invitation on the ground that his church was not of foreign origin. For the time being the Japanese accepted his contention, but in January 1942 the Chairman of the Society sent a personal representative to see Mr. Wang at the Tabernacle to urge him to join the Society; he also carried a warning as to the consequences if he were to refuse. Mr. and Mrs. Wang and three fellow-workers, realizing the critical nature of the situation they faced, asked for time to reply—time which was spent in prayer for divine guidance. As they prayed the words of 2 Corinthians 6.14, "Be ye not unequally yoked together with unbelievers", seemed to force themselves on his mind and they stopped praying. Instead the group gave themselves to praise and thanksgiving to God. The five had reached their decision. "We will not join!" And the messenger was informed of this decision. For several months nothing further happened, but in May a Japanese Christian minister in Peking, the Rev. Odakamo, strongly urged Mr. Wang to desist from the course he was pursuing and warned him again of the likely consequences if he did not.

May in Peking is the month when all is beautiful; the crowds flock to the Central Park and the Palace Lakes to view the flowers and to enjoy the warm sunshine after the long bitter winter, but in May 1942 dark clouds were massing on the horizon for the Chinese Church and Mr. Wang knew it. On the 29th of May he preached in the Tabernacle on the subject of "The Four Saints who passed through the Lion's Den and the Fiery Furnace". This was virtually his answer to the Japanese pastor. In spite of the threat to the Tabernacle and its probable closure, and in spite of fears for his aged mother, his helpless wife and his young son, and in spite of the knowledge of his own probable arrest by the ruthless Japanese military police, he had firmly made up his mind. After a severe inner struggle his answer was, "No, we will not join the new union of churches."

His letter of refusal was passed on to a Japanese official called Kono whose address and telephone number Mr. Wang knew. There were those who urged him to see Kono and explain his position in order to clear away misunderstanding. But his wife said that after making his decision this would be a sign of weakness and would show that he was afraid of the Japanese, which would be inconsistent with his repeated emphasis on not being afraid of man. Daily he expected to be visited by the Japanese authorities, but they kept him in suspense week after week. It was not until the Chinese National Day on October 10th that Mr. Wang was summoned to a discussion at the Japanese Cultural Investigation Bureau. Early that morning a few Christians met to pray about the interview, realizing how critical it was likely to be. At the appointed time Mr. Wang rode off on his bicycle to fulfil his appointment, singing "Onward, Christian soldiers".

The Japanese official Takeda said politely, "On October 15th the North China Chinese Christian Church Fellowship will be inaugurated. Both Chinese and Japanese Christian leaders very much hope that you will agree to participate in the leadership of the new organization." Mr. Wang courteously but firmly replied, "On principle, the Tabernacle cannot associate itself with any organization or establishment." Then Takeda said sternly, "But the Japanese government has decided on the unification of all the churches and this must be achieved." To which Mr. Wang replied, "As I obey the Lord whom I have served and as I keep the Truth which I have believed, I will not obey any man's command that goes against the will of God. I have already prepared myself to pay any price and make any sacrifice but I will not change the decision I have made."

Strangely enough, when Mr. Wang refused to discuss the matter any further, the Japanese authorities ceased to trouble him or the Tabernacle, though they did succeed in installing a man as the Wangs' gatekeeper whose job it was to spy on the activities of the Tabernacle. Before long, however, those activities led to the gatekeeper's conversion!

Mr. Wang, fearing that he might be faced with the death penalty, as so many others who refused to obey orders had been, had even ordered a coffin to be made and stored in the home—just in case! He was indeed "a man of iron", who, like John the Baptist, was always ready to pay the ultimate penalty in defence of his principles and what he believed to be the will of God for him. In this first major confrontation with authority God did not require his sacrifice and he continued his popular and powerful ministry right through the years of war until peace came at last in 1945. Among the close friends of those years was Pastor David Yang of Shansi, who spent most of the war years in Peking, and was one of the few guest preachers ever to be invited to preach in the Tabernacle. Some neutral foreigners from Norway and Sweden who continued to reside in Peking also attended his church and supported him with their prayers. During the war, travel was naturally restricted, but Mr. Wang was nevertheless able to visit some churches in occupied north China.

7 *On the Crest of a Wave*

The strain of those war years had been great and when conditions were relaxed in 1945 Mr. Wang Ming-dao not unnaturally experienced a physical reaction. For the first time in his ministry he suffered a period of ill-health, but he was not out of action for long. Although his Peking congregation was bursting at the seams and experiencing a new influx of university students, he could not say "No" to the flood of invitations that began to reach him from all over China. In 1946 he visited West China to hold convention meetings in Szechwan. Then his mother fell ill and he wa; kept busy in Peking until her death in 1947. The old home now became the office for *Spiritual Food Quarterly*.

The war with Japan ended, civil war between the Nationalists and Communists had tragically been renewed, in spite of General Marshall's attempts to mediate between the two parties. The overall political situation soon became chaotic. Whole areas of north China came under Communist control. The demoralized Nationalist armies were no match for the well-disciplined, well-trained Communist forces, and territories controlled by the Nationalists steadily shrank. Manchuria fell and soon Peking was threatened. The ideological conflict was reflected most acutely in the student world and not least in Peking where a bitter struggle went on. Communist student leaders were arrested and executed. Communist inspired demonstrations led to bloodshed as the police opened fire on the demonstrators. Similar incidents were taking place all over China. For the Nationalists, the writing was on the wall.

Against this sombre background a remarkable spiritual movement was taking place in the universities. Its origins lay in the evangelism among refugee students in west, south-west and north-west China during the war. In 1945 at a delegate conference held in Chungking the China Inter-Varsity Fellowship was inaugurated. Thus, when the war came to an end and the universities hurried back to their original homes, many of them became for the first time centres of an evangelical Christian witness led by converted students. It was a movement of the Holy Spirit of God and it grew spontaneously. The Second National Conference of Evangelical Students was held in Nanking in July 1947 and attracted about three hundred delegates from almost every university in China. Pastor David Yang, Calvin Chao, Mr. Andrew Gih and the venerable Dr. Jia Yu-ming were the speakers. Among the delegates were four from Peking.

Peking was becoming the scene of a remarkable work of God. In July–August, 1946, David Adeney had been present at a prayer conference for students held in the Tabernacle. This was followed by an evangelistic campaign in the Salvation Army Citadel at which Mr. Wang was the evangelist. Many conversions resulted. At first the small Christian groups in the fifteen colleges and universities were scarcely aware of one another. But when a Christian lady offered her spacious home for the use of students and resident missionary "advisers", united meetings became possible. Thanks to several outstanding student leaders the work was soon well organized. Regular fellowship meetings began to attract upwards of a hundred and fifty young people every Sunday morning at 8 o'clock before church time. A "wall-newspaper" recorded the multiplying activities of all the unions as well as of the central fellowship which adopted the name of "Peking Fellowship of Christian Students". Incidentally, it elected to remain independent of the new China I.V.F. In 1947, without any financial backing and despite the sheer poverty of most of the students, the Fellowship decided to hold its own local summer

conference, in August. The venue was some ram-
shackle buildings which had once been the Emperor's
stables, outside the Summer Palace walls. There were
neither tables nor beds. Everyone slept on straw
palliasses on the floor and the simple food was served
on makeshift trestles. But no one who was present
will ever forget that glorious week. The main
speakers were Pastor David Yang from Shanghai and
Mr. Wang Ming-dao, who, typically, spoke on the
subject of "Sin", "The Virgin Birth", "The Cross",
"The Resurrection" and "The Second Coming".
After four days it was evident that the Holy Spirit
was at work. Several students accepted Christ as
Saviour. The Christian students were experiencing
liberty in prayer. And as one after another began to
meet with the Lord in a new way, "revival" was
the only word to describe what happened. Mr.
Andrew Gih of the Bethel Band, who was visiting
Peking for other meetings, called in at the conference
and many offered themselves for Christian service in
response to his stirring appeal. It was another great
day and the final testimony meeting went on for
hours as the students poured out their hearts in
thanksgiving for what God had done in their lives.
There is no question but that the impact of Mr.
Wang Ming-dao's preaching had had a profound
effect and his individual counselling of students had
been enormously appreciated. As the conference
ended, truck-loads of students returned to Peking
singing as they went. Peking, long familiar with
student movements and demonstrations, had never
before witnessed students so spontaneously and
unashamedly demonstrating for Christ.

In late January and early February 1948 the
student centre in the city was crowded for a week of

meetings. The spiritual atmosphere was warm and there was much intense prayer. Sometimes it seemed dangerously emotional, but God was in control and, in the light of the deteriorating political situation and the knowledge that very soon Communism must prevail, the deep sincerity, the zeal and the courage of these young people was tremendously impressive. Mr. Wang Ming-dao was again the chief speaker, this time warning against those in the church whom he called "false prophets". It was another memorable conference, characterized by the almost incessant sound of prayer between the meetings from every available room in the house. Here were young people, knowing that the future held only great trials, who were determined to get to know God in a real and deep way. In every college they were already being challenged by their left-wing fellow-students. Indeed, the leadership of the Peking Student Christian Fellowship even experimented with the Communist style "self-criticism" meetings for the leaders. The result was vaguely reminiscent of the early days of the Oxford Group Movement.

As the summer of 1948 approached, the students made plans for a second summer retreat. This time Mr. Calvin Chao, the chief founder of the China I.V.F., came from Nanking to be the main speaker. Mr. Xu Hung-dao, a well known Tientsin pastor, was another of the speakers and he gave a series each evening on the Song of Songs. August 7th was Mr. Wang Ming-dao's wedding anniversary when he recalled the story of his engagement and, for the benefit of the young people, high-lighted the lessons of his twenty years of married life. Mr. Wang was greatly loved and held in high esteem by the students. His manliness, his forthrightness, his clear uncompromising exposition of biblical Christianity, and his past record of courage were all alike admired. He was indeed their hero. Many of them attended the Tabernacle faithfully every Sunday, even though it sometimes meant listening to the service relayed to an overflow room or the courtyard outside. Like Mr. Watchman Nee in Shanghai, Mr. Wang was at the peak of his popularity and career. In 1950 he published his autobiography *These Fifty Years*, a remarkable record of God's faithfulness. He would soon have every reason to put that faithfulness to the test once again. Dark days lay ahead.

8 *Second Confrontation*

In 1948 President Chiang Kai-shek paid a visit to Peking to admire the "red leaves of autumn" in the beautiful Western Hills. It was his final farewell to that ancient capital, for beyond the Western Hills and the Great Wall of China the Communist armies were massing for their final onslaught, which would soon bring them overwhelming victory over the Nationalist armies. Peking fell in January 1949 and on October 1st was proclaimed the new capital of the People's Republic of China, by Chairman Mao Tse-tung.

Wang Ming-dao had always been a fighter himself —for truth, for righteousness and for the Faith. He had won many a battle in his fifty years, but the greatest battles of his life were yet to come and he knew it. He was not deceived when in May 1950 Mr.

Chou En-lai, the new Premier, invited a group of leading churchmen to a three-day conference in Peking. No Chinese government had ever before shown such official interest in the Christian Church. These leaders were now asked to approve a Manifesto which contained both an admission that the Christian Church in China had been a tool of imperialism and an agreement to purge itself of all imperialist influences; moreover, the Church promised to give its first loyalty to the government and to render entire obedience to the Communist Party. On these terms the churches were left with the impression that they would enjoy that "freedom of religious belief" guaranteed in the Constitution. Mr. Wang must have looked on with dismay. For most, though not all, of these churchmen were men who had experienced the scourge of his pen or his tongue. In his view their liberal theology was a betrayal of the Christian faith and the Y.M.C.A. of which Mr. Wu Yao-tsung, the leader of the deputation, was the head, had notoriously been radical not only in its theology but also in its politics. If these were the men who were seeking co-operation with the Communist government, Mr. Wang well knew what to expect at their hands. As for him he would certainly refuse to sign the Manifesto whatever the consequences.

Wang Ming-dao's faith was firmly grounded on the rock of Holy Scripture. He believed the Scriptures, both Old and New Testaments, to be fully inspired. They were his sole rule of faith and conduct. To throw doubt on the reliability of the Scriptures was, in his eyes, a betrayal of the Christian faith and an act of disloyalty to Christ. For those who adopted the destructively critical modernist attitude to the Bible, he had nothing but scorn and never hesitated to denounce them and to warn Christians of the dangers of theological modernism in every form. He would have been proud and honoured to have been known as a fundamentalist, though he was certainly not an obscurantist. He was not one to be ashamed of fighting in defence of the fundamental doctrines of the Faith with scholarly weapons. In May 1935 Mr. Wang had taken part in a Conservative Evangelical Conference in Kaifeng, the aim of which was to present a united front against the rising tide of doctrinal infidelity in the Chinese Church. Other mighty men like Dr. Jia Yu-ming of Nanking, Chen Chi-kwei of the Changsha Bible Institute, Calvin Chao of Suchow, Leland Wang and Pastor Li of Nanking were also among the speakers. The lines were clearly drawn and the battle joined. Wang Ming-dao never ceased to speak out against every new evidence of spiritual and theological decline in the Church and his salvoes always landed on target.

Thus it was that in 1950 he could expect no quarter from his church enemies. He and Watchman Nee were very soon singled out by the leaders of the "Three-Self Patriotic Movement" as the two men who, by their nation-wide influence, symbolized the ideological opposition to them personally and to the movement as a whole. Like the Japanese in 1941, the Communists in 1951 were determined to unite all the churches under one banner, the banner of patriotism, and to bring them under firm central control. Many Christians had misgivings from the first and had little confidence in the men who went along with the government Religious Affairs Bureau in sponsoring it. But powerful forces were in support and sinister powers of persuasion were used to bring all possible dissenters into line. The majority succumbed to blandishments, fair promises, specious argument and the hopes of preserving the existence of the Church in a Communist society. Indeed, to many it seemed the only hope of this being realized. Co-operation with the government authorities was rationalized and attempts were made to justify it on biblical grounds. Many good men like the outstanding evangelical Marcus Cheng at first accepted the arguments and came to terms with their consciences and with the organization, only to realize their error later and confess it. There were also other good men who stayed with the movement until the end. But Wang Ming-dao from his biblical standpoint saw very clearly from the beginning the true nature of Communism. He was convinced that compromise was not the way to glorify God nor save the Church. Once more "the man of iron" steeled himself for the approaching ordeal. He harboured no illusions about the outcome, but took courage and comfort from the example of Martin Luther.

In 1951 many Christians were arrested and fear dominated the Christian community as one after another prominent Christian was "accused" and punished. The press conducted a violent campaign of abuse against the Church and individual Christians. In May 1952 Watchman Nee was arrested, tried and sentenced to twenty years' imprisonment. One arch-enemy was out of the way: when would the turn of the other come? But Wang Ming-dao refused to be intimidated. In the November 1951 issue of *Spiritual Food Quarterly*, which he continued to distribute, he wrote, "In 1927 I already knew that if in this present time I faithfully proclaimed the Word of God—rebuking the sins, the evils and the doctrine-destroying teachings in the

I

corrupted nominal church—I should surely meet the
opposition and persecution which met Martin
Luther. . . . The one who faithfully preaches the
Word of God cannot but expect to meet opposition
in the form of malicious slander and abuse from some
leaders in the Church and from 'Christians' who are
spiritually dead. I know that this will come to pass,
I am prepared to meet it. I covet the courage and
faithfulness of Martin Luther, therefore I again in
this issue reprint his prayer:

> 'Almighty and Eternal God, how fearful is this
> world as it bares its great teeth to eat one up! How
> weak is my heart as it rests in Thee! . . . I have no
> quarrel with the rulers of this world . . . but the
> affairs of this day are for Thy cause . . . I pray
> Thee, for the sake of Thy beloved Son, Jesus
> Christ, be at my side. He is my Fortress, He is my
> Shield, He also is my Defence. Now I am prepared
> and ready—ready to give my life for Thy Truth
> . . . though the world be filled with devils;
> though for punishment they put me in the stocks
> and tear me to pieces or cut me up; yes, though
> they burn me to ashes, yet is my life with Thee . . .
> Amen. O God I pray Thee help me. Amen.'"

In this spirit Wang Ming-dao continued to declare
publicly from his pulpit that the Church cannot come
to terms with the world without compromise and
that a Church entangled with this world's policies and
politics and which has become a mere servant of an
atheist government has ceased to function as the true
Church of Jesus Christ. Between 1951 and 1954 he
published a spate of books on various aspects of this
theme. Thus Mr. Wang became increasingly an

embarrassment to the leaders of the Three-Self Movement and a major hindrance to progress in the task assigned to them by the government.

In the spring of 1954, therefore, the Three-Self Movement, professedly a spontaneous Christian organization, sent out a circular to all the churches and Christian organizations in Peking requiring them to appoint delegates to attend a meeting at which Mr. Wang Ming-dao was to be publicly "accused". Reports say that there was great excitement at the meeting as many people raised their voices at the same time. Mr. Wang, the accused, for his part, sat quietly on the platform, his eyes fixed on the ceiling, never uttering a word. Following the accusations, the chairman asked the delegates whether they recommended death or prison. But only a quarter of those present assented to either. The rest sat silent, some weeping, and no punishment was decreed.

Several days later Mr. Wang's Christian student friends daringly started an "Oppose the Persecution of Wang Ming-dao" campaign, which immediately received wide support from Peking churches and Christian organizations. The protest spread to Tientsin and Shanghai and was reported all over China by the daily press.

For several weeks after the "accusation" meeting Mr. Wang did not preach at the Tabernacle but gave himself to prayer, to writing and to personal interviews in his own home. No printer would any longer dare to print his magazine and so he had to set up his own type and print his own editions of *Spiritual Food Quarterly*—a task which kept him working late at nights. When he resumed preaching it was to larger crowds than ever and in January 1955 the best attended evangelistic meetings he had ever conducted resulted in many conversions.

In May, the Three-Self Movement held its fourth annual conference in Peking, attended by six hundred delegates from all branches of the Christian Church. The leaders decided to make one last effort to win over Wang Ming-dao. Six of the Movement's most prominent men called to see him at his home, but he refused to meet them. Were they not the very men who had had him tried in 1954? Angered, the Three-Self Movement ordered "accusation meetings" to be held all over China against him. On July 25th, forty-nine responsible Christian leaders meeting in Hankow vented their spleen on their colleague. This new campaign happened to coincide with the campaign of abuse against Hu Feng, a well-known Communist writer who had been expelled from the Communist Party for his views. So Wang Ming-dao and Hu Feng shared a dubious notoriety in the national press. Every kind of opprobrium was heaped upon the lone Peking hero. On July 31st the official church publication, *Heavenly Wind*, contained an open attack on Wang Ming-dao and listed all his "crimes". Only his personal character escaped attack.

Undeterred and undismayed by the storm that was raging about him, Mr. Wang calmly conducted another two weeks of meetings during July, with record attendances and then went away to Bei-dai-he with his wife for a two weeks' seaside holiday. On his return home he issued another *Spiritual Food Quarterly*, several reprints of his books, for which there was an incessant demand, and two pamphlets which were highly controversial: *Truth or Poison* and *Loyalty to God without respect of persons*. The first was an analysis of the Communist claim that the teaching of

missionaries was "imperialist poison". Though Mr.
Wang held no brief for missionaries, he successfully
demonstrated that their alleged "poisonous doctrines"
were in fact the fundamental doctrines of Christianity. His closing words were, "In conclusion, a word
to the saints: in the Scriptures there is nothing but
the pure truth of God, without any 'imperialist
poison' . . . : we must go on believing and preaching
it . . . we are ready to pay any price to preserve the
Word of God and we are equally willing to sacrifice
anything in order to preach the Word of God . . .
Don't give way, don't compromise! The battle is
indeed furious, the battlefield full of dangers, but
God's glory will be manifest there. He will honour
them who honour Him . . . the trumpet has been
blown. The victory is in sight. My dear brothers and
sisters, let us follow in the steps of the Lord and,
holding aloft His banner, go forward courageously
for His gospel's sake."

The second pamphlet was a clear challenge to all
Christians to take a firm stand for Christ. Leaders of
the Three-Self Movement immediately criticized
Mr. Wang during the course of public worship and
in articles in the press. It was clear that the crisis was
near. Mr. Wang must be finally silenced. His free
speaking had been tolerated long enough. Sensing
that events were moving fast, Wang Ming-dao
preached what proved to be his last sermon on
August 7th. Knowing that he might be arrested any
day, the text of that sermon was "The Son of man is
betrayed into the hands of sinners"—a pointed
reference to what Wang Ming-dao believed to be the
betrayal of Christ by the self-appointed and govern-
ment-sponsored representatives of the Church in
China. At the end of the service Mr. Wang had copies

of his own personal manifesto, *We, because of our faith* . . . distributed to the congregation. In this pamphlet he expounded his views that present events were but a continuation of the old familiar conflict between those who held to the authority of God's Word in faith and practice and those who minimized the authority of Holy Scriptures and set themselves up as critics. The concluding words of the document were, ". . . regardless of how many others may twist the truth and slander us, we, because of our faith will remain steadfast".

Wang Ming-dao did not have long to wait. Soon after midnight the police called and ordered Mr. and Mrs. Wang to dress. They were then bound with ropes and escorted to the prison. Eighteen young Christians of college age who were members of the Tabernacle congregation were also arrested at the same time. Mr. Wang had never on principle uttered a word of criticism of the government as such but only of the Three-Self Movement, the official church organization. In spite of this, he and the others were charged with resistance to the government and Mr. Wang was given a fifteen-year prison sentence. A letter written by a loyal follower of Mr. Wang on the day of his arrest quoted Luke 23.2, "They began to accuse him, saying, We found this fellow perverting the nation. . . ."

Mr. Wang's place in the Tabernacle pulpit was taken by one of his colleagues. But a week or two later he also was arrested and the Tabernacle was closed and sealed. The voice which had for so long boldly witnessed to the Truth amid the babel voices of error and compromise was silenced at last.

9 *The Agony*

The Communists and their allies in the churches were determined to wring from this courageous man the final humiliation. Throughout August and September he was subject to intense brainwashing—incessant discussion, argument and debate and the now familiar psychological pressures used with such effect in the Communist world. Mr. Wang finally cracked and put his signature to a document written to satisfy all the demands of his inquisitors. It began, "I am a person guilty of anti-revolutionary deeds. I am obliged to the patient education of the government which made me realize my own mistakes, and yet the government dealt with me genuinely and has delivered me from the deep gulf of crime," and concluded with the words "concerning my criminal deeds I have now confessed to the government the whole matter frankly." On the strength of this document Mr. Wang was released from prison on September 30th and read his public confession before a large meeting of Three-Self Movement delegates. *Heavenly Wind*, now the voice of the Movement, hailed Mr. Wang's recantation as a great victory—but it proved to be a hollow one.

Mr. Wang Ming-dao, after his intense ordeal, began to show signs of severe strain. He became mentally deranged and was heard to go about saying, "I am Peter" or at times "I am Judas". He felt that he had denied and betrayed his Lord whom he had served so loyally and so courageously for so many years. Finally, as reason returned, Mr. and Mrs. Wang decided to inform the Communist authorities that his statement had been made under duress and in no way represented his own true convictions. Mr. Wang was immediately returned to prison.

Since then little has been heard of this prisoner for Christ. It is known that his fifteen years' sentence was extended to a life sentence. In 1967 a letter to his sister-in-law reached Hong Kong, "I am very well and happy. Please be of good cheer. My feelings are just the same as yours. You must be glad to hear this. All things work together for good. Be of good cheer, I am much more precious than sparrows." In 1970 he was moved from Peking to a correction or labour camp in Dadong, north Shansi. There he remains—the man whose life spans seventy-two years of change and revolution in China, and of turmoil, strife and renewal in the Church.

"Chief among the Three"

David Yang, Watchman Nee and Wang Ming-dao were friends who respected one another. In age they were virtually contemporaries, two being born in 1900 and one in 1902. They all emerged and witnessed amidst the strains of national and religious life in China in the first half of the twentieth century. All were outside the work of the mainline denominations. While all three made a significant contribution to the total life of the Christian Church in China, each man was also a distinct personality different from the others and the contribution each was able to make was different in kind.

Wang Ming-dao was a native of Peking, the charming capital of China of both ancient and modern times and the symbol of Chinese culture, but also a hotbed of anti-West feeling. There he grew up at the heart of the empire, there he was educated, there he lived and served Christ, only leaving it to undertake his long evangelistic journeys, and there in the end in the capital of Communist China he met the fierce opposition of the enemies of Christ.

Watchman Nee, too, was a city man. He was in fact a man of two cities—the two treaty ports of Foochow and Shanghai—where he spent his whole life under the shadow of "foreign imperialism" and, as far as Shanghai is concerned, amid sophistication and materialism. He knew little of life in rural China.

David Yang, on the contrary, was a country lad

born and brought up in the comparatively primitive
and poverty-stricken environment of an inland
province far from the coast. No culture or sophistication surrounded him in his early years.

Wang of Peking owed little to foreign missionaries.
Nee of Foochow owed much to individual foreigners,
though little to missionary institutions. Yang of
Shansi, however, owed everything to the work of
foreign missions—his family's conversion to Christianity, his education, his own conversion, his
theological and church training, his early sphere of
service, the encouragement to embark on his own first
independent venture and the opportunity to teach in
a missionary theological college.

It is not surprising, therefore, that David Yang
never adopted an anti-missionary stance, for his own
experience had let him see the best in Missions. Nor
is it really surprising that Watchman Nee, with his
very different experiences of missionary institutions
and living in two of the most anti-foreign cities of
China, should have been drawn into independency
and a critical attitude towards Missions. Wang
Ming-dao, though critical of the missionary movement in general, never isolated himself from it and
his positive ministry was welcome in almost all
denominations and churches throughout China.

While Wang Ming-dao was the founder and leader
of a congregation in Peking, he never so much as
contemplated starting a movement or encouraging
others to follow his example. He was in no sense a
separatist. And so, unlike Watchman Nee, who
created deep schism among the churches of China
and thereby restricted his usefulness and his ministry
largely to his own sectarian group, David Yang and
Wang Ming-dao served all the churches without

prejudice, without exception and with great acceptance. Both contributed greatly to the widespread renewal and the upbuilding of the whole Church. Though friendly admirers of Watchman Nee, they were alike critical of his extreme and exclusive views which set up Little Flock churches as the only true churches. Every movement which is dominated by individual personalities without full safeguards against "private interpretation" of Scripture exposes itself to doctrinal vagaries and the disruption which they produce. The Little Flock in China—and more recently overseas—has not escaped these dangers. Only within some credal framework, some doctrinal consensus, can the Church be protected against the "private interpretation" and the dogmatic control of individuals with a charisma that makes them leaders.

In the sphere of literature, the periodicals of Watchman Nee and Wang Ming-dao had a nation-wide circulation and acceptance. But it was Wang Ming-dao who published the greatest number of books in China. Unlike the books associated with Watchman Nee which have appeared in the West, Wang Ming-dao's writings have yet to be translated and published outside China and are therefore little known. Their great value lay in the manner in which the author showed how the Christian life should be lived out practically in the pagan and materialistic society of China. Watchman Nee's books with all their rich spirituality often border on the mystical and in some respects seem strangely unrelated to the problems of living in the real world of China then and now.

Together all three men speak with authority to a wider public than the Christian world of China in the troubled first half of this century.

1. *The local church*

All three saw clearly the Pauline truth of the Church, local and universal. But they all reacted against the importation from the West of our denominational confusion. They longed to see a truly Chinese pattern of church life firmly based on the New Testament concept of the Body of Christ. One or other may have reacted too strongly against the missionary churches, but were they to be blamed? Was not the blame rather on the inadequate doctrine of the Church as understood and taught by missionaries as a whole? At New Delhi in 1961 the World Council of Churches coined the expression "all in each place" to describe the nature of the Church. If missionaries in China had had a better appreciation of New Testament Church truth, there would probably have been less reaction against the missionary movement there. Possibly only local churches on the New Testament pattern will be able to preserve their inner vitality in the catacombs of present-day China.

2. *Sanctification*

All three men were exponents of the necessity and the secret of holy or Christ-like living. Nee and Yang emphasized the inwardness of the sanctified life while Wang never ceased to hammer home the need for an outward expression of practical holiness in every sphere of life. In an age of laxity and permissiveness even within the Christian community these men would have stood out on any convention platform in the West as men with a message, and a message that would have brought us to our knees in humility and repentance for our subnormal standards of Christian conduct.

3. *Revival*

All three men preached about revival, not as a theory but as something they knew about in their own personal experience. They had been involved in and observant of the revival movements of the 1920's and 1930's—their blessings and their dangers, the true and the false. They spoke and wrote about what they knew. Each had had what today might be called a "charismatic" experience, but it is safe to say that none would have belonged to a "charismatic movement". The sanctifying work of the Holy Spirit, the Spirit's ninefold fruit and the varied gifts of the Spirit would all have had a prominent place in their teaching, but they were well aware that revival has not always historically been associated with an emphasis on "tongues speaking" and none of the three made this an issue of first importance in their revival ministry.

4. *Suffering*[1]

All three men suffered much for Christ. All, especially Nee and Yang, often preached about the place of suffering in the Christian life, not as something to be avoided if possible but as something to be welcomed in so far as it was a fellowship in the sufferings of Christ. As St. Paul makes plain in 2 Corinthians 4, and St. Peter in his first epistle, suffering is the inevitable pathway for everyone who would follow in the steps of a suffering Saviour. I vividly remember a message by David Yang on Revelation 1.9, "I John, your brother, who share with you in Jesus the tribulation and the kingdom and the patient

[1] Cf. *The Voice of China's Christians*, edited by A. T. F. Reynolds.

endurance . . ."(RSV), and I well recollect Watchman
Nee declaring that if a day went past when he did
not experience something of the Cross in his life he
would ask his Heavenly Father for the reason why.
As St. Peter puts it in 1 Peter 5.10, "And after you
have suffered a little while, the God of all grace . . .
will himself restore, establish, and strengthen
you"(RSV). Suffering is the price to be paid for
spiritual maturity and the highest conformity to
Christ in His death and resurrection.

Like David's three chief mighty men, each of
"China's Mighty Men" excelled in his own way. But
in strength and nobility of character and in the
extent and constructiveness of the influence which
he exercised, the "Man of Iron" must be reckoned as
"chief among the three".

Bibliography

Bush, Richard C., *Religion in Communist China* (Abingdon Press, N.Y.)

Chan, Stephen, *My Uncle, Nee To-sheng* (The Alliance Press, Hong Kong)

Clark, William H., *The Church in China* (Council Press, N.Y.)

Nee, Watchman, *The Normal Christian Church Life* (Victory Press)

—— *The Normal Christian Life* (Victory Press)

—— *The Release of the Spirit* (Sure Foundation Publishers, U.S.A.)

Paton, David N., *Christian Missions and the Judgment of God* (S.C.M.)

Patterson, George, *Christianity in Communist China* (Word Books, London and N.Y.)

Swanson, Allen J., *Taiwan—Mainland versus Independent Church Growth* (W. Carey Library, U.S.A.)

T'ong, Hollington K., *Christianity in Taiwan—a History* (China Post, Taipei)